Quilting by Improvisation

EXPLORING CURVES, OPENWORK AND DIMENSION

VIKKI PIGNATELLI

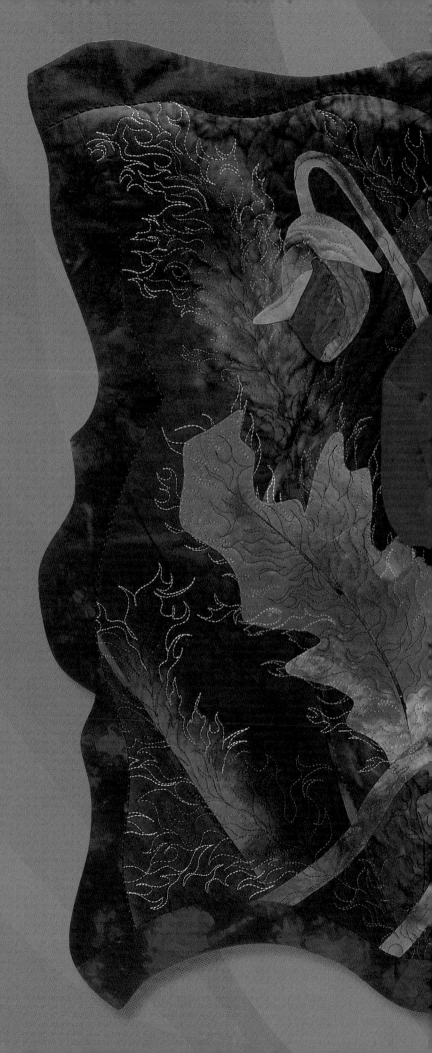

First U.S. Edition published in 2006
© Vikki Pignatelli

Publisher:
Linda Chang Teufel

Graphic Design:
Kimberly Koloski

Illustrations:
Vikki Pignatelli, Kimberly Koloski

Photographer:
Larry Friar

Copy Editor:
Patricia Radloff

Technical Editor:
Augustine Ellis

Author's assistant for illustrations:
Rhonda Pfahler

Consultant for color chapter:
Diana Seebode, MFA, PhD

Author Photo:
Vincent Photography, Dublin, Ohio

Publisher's Cataloging in Publication Data

Pignatelli, Vikki
Quilting by Improvisation:
Exploring Curves, Openwork
and Dimension
1.Quilting
2.Machine quilting
I.Title
ISNB# 0-9641201-9-4

Printed in Thailand
9   8   7   6   5   4   3   2

The information in this book is presented
in good faith, but no warranty is given nor
results guaranteed. Dragon Threads as-
sumes no responsibility for the use of this
information.

Dragon Threads
490 Tucker Drive
Worthington, OH 43085
www.dragonthreads.com

Dedication

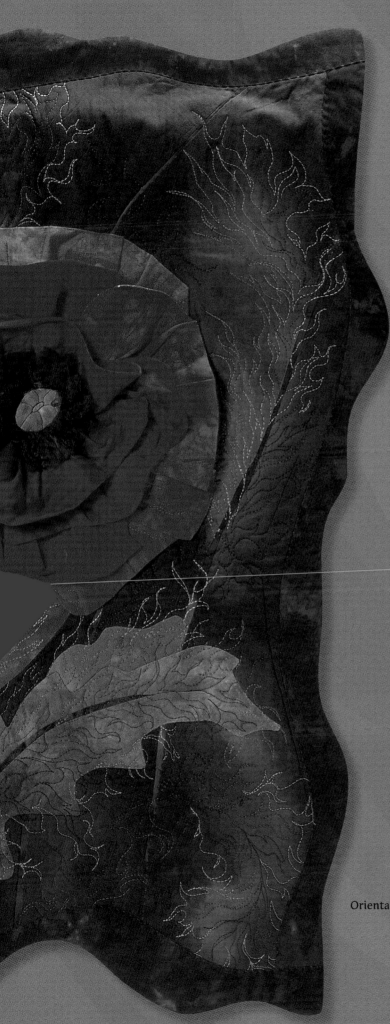

This book is dedicated to the sacred and creative Spirit that dwells within each of us, inspiring our distinctive talents and abilities to touch the minds and hearts of others with a magnitude greater than we can dream.

Oriental Poppy

Valley of Fire
Collection of
Denise and Joe Roy

Acknowledgments

An author may write the words, but it takes the involvement of many people to turn the text into a book. I would like to express my appreciation to all those who encouraged and worked with me during this exciting journey.

To Dragon Threads and Linda Teufel, a terrific editor and friend for her expertise, advice and direction with *Quilting By Improvisation*. Linda, it's been a magnificent experience working with you, creating this book and watching it evolve. You made the experience fun and are a joy as a person and an editor!

To my sister, Augustine Ellis. You encouraged me to simplify, simplify, and simplify my text and then dutifully listened to my grumbling after I needed to revise and rewrite the same chapters over and over. Words of gratitude cannot suffice for your patience, emotional support, input and inestimable assistance with the editing and positive critique of my manuscript, even at a moment's notice or anytime of the day or night.

To a fellow quiltmaker and friend, Rhonda Pfahler, for your contribution, skill, verbal input and weeks of your time while helping me construct the photographic illustration samples for this book. Rhonda, it has been a delight working side by side with you, brainstorming ideas and exploring our imaginations.

Many thanks to Diana Seebode, MFA,PhD, for your direction, consultation and encouragement during the writing of my chapter, "Color Your Quilt Beautiful." Diana, your invaluable advice and guidance is deeply appreciated!

To Kim Koloski, for your terrific abilities in graphic design and layout of *Quilting By Improvisation*. Your expertise made this book come alive!

To my students who are so generous with their love, kindness, encouragement and support. I am always awed and inspired by your warmth and creativity!

To the vendors who have supplied me with materials to illustrate this book. I appreciate your generosity more than I can say.

And finally, my deepest gratitude and affection to my husband, Denny, for your love, support and patience, especially for putting up with missed meals, a messy house, and all the craziness I've put you through not only for this past busy year, but the last thirty eight! Thank you for all the love and emotional support you give me!

Vikki Pignatelli

July, 2006

Contents

Dedication 3

Acknowlegments 5

Introduction
The Capricious Art
of Improvisation. 8

1 Preparation: quilting supplies & tools 13
Tools and supplies. 14

Thread 17

Fabric 18

2 Color your quilt beautiful 21
Elements of design 22

The properties of color . . . 23

Color schemes
& combinations 26

Shading & highlights 30

Blending 32

Color balance 33

Contrast. 35

3 Crazy About Curves basic technique 41
My Star Dances. 42

Interpreting
pattern markings 42

Marking a template
for movement 43

Lining a patch 45

Clipping curves 46

Stitching 48

Turning under straight
edges and corners. 49

Enlarging the
stabilizer foundation 50

4 Improvisational quilts 53

Making an improvisational
block quilt 54

Constructing a
freeform basic block 58

Sewing down the patches . . . 60

Making linings for
light-valued
improvisational patches 63

Making circular and oval
shaped blocks 64

Splicing seams 69

Improvisational
sheer overlay 73

5 Exploring dimension 79

Fabric manipulations 81

Choosing fabric
for manipulations 82

Simple strips 85

Multi-fabric strip units 86

Freeform pleats 89

Making tubes 93

Wrinkling and folding a
whole-cloth fabric 103

Facing shapes & patches . . . 107

Portrait of a Poppy 115

6 New explorations: making openings in your quilt 122

English Ivy 124

Alternate method for
making openings 130

Random improvisational
openings 133

Working with openings in
your own design 134

Latticework 137

7 Improvisational borders, finishes and bindings 147

Border options 149

Finishing 153

Envelope finish 156

Binding options 158

Hanging sleeve
with easement 164

Pattern templates 166

Resources 169

About the author 170

Awards 172

Artist's statements 174

Quilts 175

The capricious art of improvisation

Improvisational quilting is the freedom to create without boundaries. There are no rules, only guidelines. Improvisation is a journey and along the way there are a number of paths you may choose to explore. Keep a flexible, open mind and be prepared for adventure, for the path you follow may twist and detour many times before you reach your final destination of a completed quilt. Above all, remember that the journey itself is as important as the quilt, so relax, have fun and enjoy the experience. To give you an idea of the capricious art of improvisation, here is the story of my journey with my quilt, *The Promise of Spring*.

The Promise of Spring was made entirely using improvisational techniques. The quilt is a testament to projects that take on lives of their own. The final outcome of this quilt is not what I envisioned when I started it.

The only design idea in mind when beginning the project was to make a small or medium-sized quilt comprised of a few oval blocks. After making two blocks, I was excited to see they reminded me of rippling rings of water, as in a pond. Having a particular fondness for ponds, I made nine blocks in all, even incorporating some sheer fabrics in a variety of colors to heighten the illusion of rippling water. Not willing to eliminate any of the nine blocks, I joined them together to form a quilt top.

The way the rings rippled outward suggested something was touching or dragging in the water, so I added the vertical dangling and swaying willow branches, the tip of each branch touching the center of a water ring. Something was still not right. The branches, dropping from the top of the quilt, had no support or source of origin and looked lost and incomplete. At that point, I added a large, horizontal tree branch and lighter value pond patches above that (to give the illusion of depth and distance), extending the size and the top of the growing quilt.

Although the large branch helped to explain the presence of the smaller, swaying branches, the quilt still seemed incomplete to me. The large branch came from nowhere and cut across the quilt, dissecting it in two. The quilt also lacked flow. This time I decided to add more of the tree, constructing vertical tree trunk patches on the left side of the quilt.

Again, the tree trunk improved the design of the quilt, but the tree cried out for more. It wanted roots. I gave the tree its roots, and also added the bank of the pond, grass and dimensional flowers. Only then was I allowed to finally stop and call it a finished quilt.

So you see, quilts must evolve during the creative process to become what they want and need to be. Your job is to be flexible, take leaps of faith during the creative process and use your hands and skills to help the work become a reality and grow into a beautiful quilt.

Regarding construction of the quilt, all of the techniques I used for *The Promise of Spring* are described in the chapters in this book. The nine oval blocks were made as described on page 64 and joined together as a quilt top in the same manner as are all improvisational blocks (see page 68).

8

9

The Promise of Spring

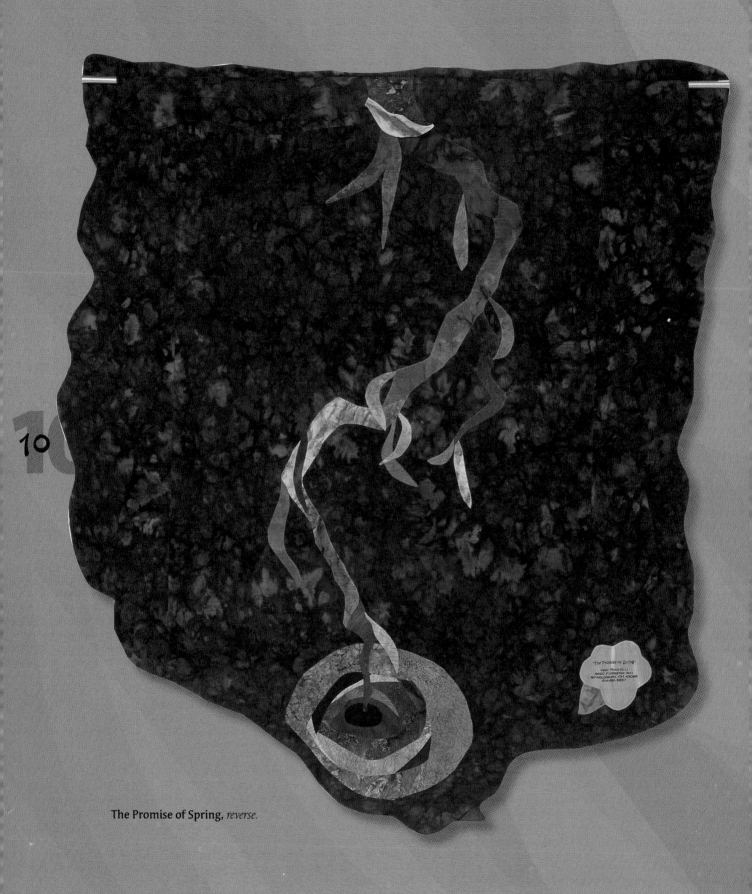

10

The Promise of Spring, *reverse.*

QUILTING BY IMPROVISATION

Once the oval blocks were joined together, I began adding the lighter, horizontal patches of "pond" above them in sequence, with each successive patch overlapping the previous one. After stitching down all the bottom pond patches (below the large horizontal tree branch), I added the dangling, swaying vertical branches.

The quilt was constructed on a stabilizer foundation. Because the size of the quilt continually grew beyond my expectations, I needed to add on to the existing stabilizer several times. (See enlarging stabilizer, page 50).

Working on a design board, the remaining elements in the quilt, such as branches, tree trunk, upper pond area, roots and bank were constructed by randomly cutting individual patches of fabric, turning under the appropriate seam allowance, and overlapping the raw edges of previously laid patches in sequence (Chapters 3 and 4).

I drew templates on freezer paper for each of the branches to use as a guideline during construction. I chose to use templates for assurance that the branches would be long enough, be pleasantly shaped and would hang correctly in relation to the corresponding water ring. The seam allowances were turned under along both long edges (sides) on the swaying branches before the branches were pinned to the top of the pond patches in the quilt top and stitched down.

The patches for the large horizontal branch, the remaining light-valued pond patches, tree trunk, roots and bank were cut improvisationally. Their seam allowances were clipped and turned under. They were layered in sequence as usual, with the turned under seam allowance of each succeeding patch covering the raw edges of a previously laid patch.

The three-dimensional willow leaves were made as described on page 112. The raw edges at the top of each leaf are tucked and hidden under overlapping tree branch patches. When the tree branch patches were sewn, the stitches also secured the leaves in place.

The dimensional flowers and leaves on the bank were made as described on page 109 and attached to the surface of the quilt. The quilt was sandwiched and free-motion quilted. I quilted the pond and trees with watery and wood-like motifs that suggested these elements. I also quilted several long, swaying ghost branches and leaves on the pond between the pieced branches.

I finished *The Promise of Spring* using a faced binding to the back. (see page 158). As the last step, I beaded the centers of the flowers and also added a few beads to some areas in the water rings to enhance the illusive effect of rippling water.

Are you ready to start your own journey? Pack your favorite fabrics and color combinations. You don't need to bring money with you, just excitement and a sense of wonder. As with any trip, set out to have fun and don't worry about what might happen along the way. The ideas presented in this chapter, or the entire book for that matter, represent all the different paths you can follow. Take time to explore each path and enjoy every journey.

11

Preparation:
Supplies & Tools

Most quilters will have on hand the quilting supplies needed for the techniques described in this book. Keep in mind as you purchase tools, supplies, fabrics and threads to invest in well-made, reliable items. Using high grade fabrics and tools makes your quilting life easier because they work accurately and consistently. Quality is especially important when considering fabrics and threads.

Left, **Field Poppies**, *detail.*
Above, **He Loves Me, He Loves Me Not.**

Agood artist does not use cheap paintbrushes or paints because she/he will not achieve the best results in the finished painting. It's the same for your quiltmaking. You are an artist and fabric is your medium. Regardless of whether you are a hobbyist or a professional quiltmaker, you deserve the advantage of using the best tools and materials for your art that you can afford. It doesn't make sense to invest hours of work into a quilt but use inferior supplies.

Tools & supplies

Sewing machine

Keep your sewing machine in good working order with regular maintenance. Oil it regularly as directed by your owner's manual or as advised by your dealer. Keep your sewing machine clean. Remove the throatplate (check the manufacturer's directions) and bobbin case to clean the debris from these areas using an artist's paintbrush. Threads, lint and dust accumulate rapidly in the bobbin area and under the throatplate, affecting the stitch quality of the machine. Many stitch related problems—especially with free-motion stitching—are due to debris in and around the bobbin area.

Your sewing machine is your best companion and playmate and you need to treat it as such. In return it will give you many hours of pleasure and fun, not to mention good results. Life is good for a quilter when the sewing machine is running smoothly.

You can get more work done in a shorter amount of time and with less emotional wear and tear.

Stitches

The main stitch you'll use for the projects in the book is the blind hemstitch ∧----∧----∧. It is a standard stitch on most sewing machines. The blind hemstitch is the best choice and the least visible once the quilt is completed. If your machine does not have a blind hemstitch, you may choose a blanket stitch _ _|_ _|_ _ , a small zigzag stitch or a short-length, regular stitch on the edge of the patch. You may enjoy experimenting with some of the decorative stitches on your machine, especially for improvisational and crazy quilt-type projects.

Machine feet

Open-toe appliqué foot: Maximum range of view while stitching is essential for a quilter's self-confidence and accuracy. Use an open-toe appliqué foot for the blind hemstitch, even if your owner's manual suggests using another type of foot for the blind hemstitch function. If you do not have an open-toe appliqué foot I strongly suggest you consider purchasing one. It is a wonderful foot to have and well worth the expense.

Walking foot: This wonderful foot helps assure an even flow of multiple layers of fabric through the sewing machine. A walking foot is not necessary, but is helpful with this topstitch technique.

Needles

For piecing cottons and most fabrics, I use universal 80/12 machine needles. For free-motion quilting, I strongly recommend using 90/14 topstitch machine needles. These needles have an elongated eye, easing the friction on the thread caused by the

14

continuous stitching motion during the quilting process. Thread breakage can occur if the needle's eye is too small.

Needles are inexpensive considering the job they do. Change them often. They become dull quickly or can develop burrs on the tip or eye that will snag the fabric in your quilt or cause your thread to fray as you stitch. I change my needles (both regular stitching and quilting) after every few hours of sewing.

Stabilizer

Non-woven, non-stretch stabilizer is an essential item for topstitch appliqué. It is used as a foundation for the patches in the quilt top during the construction process and remains in the quilt permanently. This material should be washable and without stretch, so your quilt top remains true to shape regardless of how the patches are sewn on. Using a foundation fabric, patches can be cut out randomly without consideration of the fabric grain, giving you a great deal of freedom. If you want to utilize a particular pattern motif in the fabric, such as a leaf, or simulate motion such as rain or wind, you may cut the patch from the fabric and position the motif exactly the way you want it in the quilt. Once the patches are sewn down to the stabilizer they stay firmly in place without stretching, even if they are cut on the bias.

Additionally, using stabilizer helps the quilt to hang straight and evenly after it is finished. Foundation also adds density to the quilt, helping to stabilize the stitch tension during free-motion quilting so it is not necessary to use a hoop.

Choose a regular stabilizer. Do not buy interfacing, or fusible or tear-away products for this technique. The stabilizer brand I recommend is Pellon™, manufactured by Pellon Consumer Products. It is available in most fabric stores in the United States, Canada and Australia and the official name is "#30 (Lightweight) Stabilizer."

In countries other than those mentioned above, the counterpart of the stabilizer I use may be a variation of a product known as Vilene. If Pellon™ stabilizer is not available in your area, choose a product for the foundation that is sew-in, non-woven, non-stretch and is thick enough in weight to use as a support for your quilt top.

The important thing to look for with any material you choose to use as a foundation is whether or not it is able to withstand a hot iron. Using a foundation material that is heat sensitive will cause problems as you construct and quilt your project. Before you buy a substantial amount of any foundation material, test a small sample. Try pressing the material directly with a hot iron set on a cotton setting with steam. If there is wrinkling, shrinking or shrivel-

ing, the material is not suitable to use in your quilt and you must choose another foundation. Using a foundation material that shrivels is inviting disaster. The wrinkles will show through the fabric patches when you finish and press the quilt surface.

Stabilizer comes in different thicknesses or weights. You may choose any weight depending on the nature of your project, but for all-purpose quilting I use the light-weight (# 30) or medium-weight (#40) Pellon™ Stabilizer. If your quilt includes very heavy quilting or threadpainting, you may opt for a heavier weight stabilizer.

OESD Aqua Mesh™ water-soluble stabilizer

This product is used as a foundation to create free-stitched machine lace and latticework with decorative threads, yarns and tube manipulations. Once the sewing on the project is completed, the stitched machine lace/stabilizer is immersed in warm water. The water-soluble stabilizer dissolves completely, leaving only the web of lace. The lace may then be inserted in the openings of the quilt top.

I prefer Aqua Mesh™ because the cottony texture grabs the threads and they do not slip around while I'm sewing. With this product I do not need to use a hoop.

Batting

There are many quality battings available. Selection depends on what effect you want to achieve in your project. I use a thin, low-loft 100% cotton batting for the wall-hanging projects in this book and most of my quilts. Many times I will also use a premium grade of cotton flannel for batting. Wash and tumble dry the flannel fabric before using it as batting.

Flexible curve

This long, thin snake-like tool bends to form beautiful S-curves. Bend the tool into the curves you want, lay it on top of the drawing paper and trace the curve. The flexible curve is an essential item for any quilter who wants to design curves. It is available at quilt shops and at art and office supply stores in the drafting department. Most stores carry the tool in 12", 18" and 24" lengths. Some specialized stores (drafting supplies/architecture) carry it in 36" lengths. The 36" length is great for designing medium to large quilts. I recommend buying the 24" length or the larger size if you can find it.

Heat tool

Available in craft stores, you can use a heat tool to sear the edges of sheer fabrics, preventing fraying and creating unusual effects. A heat tool is fun to use, but the heat generated from it is intense. Take care not to burn your fingers! Read the manufacturer's directions and take all the proper precautions. When I work with this tool, I always use long needle-nosed tweezers to hold the fabric down against a Teflon™ sheet or ironing board and away from my body. The tweezers keep the fabric from blowing away and keep fingers from being burned.

Fasturn™

These inexpensive tools are specifically for turning tubes, straps and narrow strips inside out and they are a terrific item to have. They are made by Crowning Touch. I heartily recommend you purchase one—they are worth every penny. I found it spares hours of frustration!

Other tools

Besides the basic sewing supplies, other items you'll need are:

Wax paper, freezer paper and parchment paper These are available in grocery stores. Parchment paper makes a wonderful "press cloth" and doesn't scorch like fabric press cloths.

Plastic point turner or wooden skewer Used for poking out and straightening seams of projects that are turned inside out.

Drafting tape (¾" wide) Drafting tape looks like common masking tape but leaves no sticky residue on fabric or paper. It is used for joining together sheets of freezer paper, or drawing paper, during quilt top construction and it removes easily without tearing the paper. I also use it to mark the binding lines of large quilts.

Fusible web on a roll (⅝" wide) I use regular weight Stitch Witchery™ by Dritz, available in the notions department at fabric stores. It can fuse two layers of fabric together without bulk.

Dressmaker's serrated tracing wheel, rotary cutter and mat, misting bottle and needle-nosed tweezers.

16

Thread

You'll need a variety of fine quality threads in a rainbow of colors for piecing and for decorative and free-motion quilting. With the topstitch technique, all patches are stitched together on the quilt top surface. Stitching on the surface of the quilt top allows you to see and control where you sew and to make necessary adjustments to match points and straight lines. If you choose a matching or blending color of thread to sew the patch seams on the quilt top, the stitches meld with the surface fabrics and become virtually invisible.

Every technique has advantages and disadvantages. The advantages of being able to see and match your seams far outweighs having to change the top threads a bit more often. In fact, you won't be changing threads as often as you think—as you sew together the patches in the quilt top you'll find you can use the same blending thread for many of them. You do not change the bobbin thread when you change top threads.

In my classes the most frequently asked question is, "May I use invisible thread?" You certainly have the option of using invisible thread for your quilt top. Personally I have a difficult time with invisible thread and prefer the look of regular thread. I dislike the look of invisible thread and the readily visible dark needle puncture holes that are left in the fabric when sewing with invisible thread. If you choose to use invisible thread, try using a small-sized universal needle to minimize the needle puncture marks.

You may use either regular polyester or cotton thread in the bobbin. Most of the time you can leave a medium-gray thread in the bobbin because it blends with most fabrics. If you are working on a large area of dark colors such as a background, you may want to switch to black thread in the bobbin. If you are sewing with yellow or light colors, use white thread in the bobbin so the thread doesn't show or shadow on the top surface of the quilt.

For free-motion quilting, I own and use a eclectic variety of decorative threads including some rayon and twisted metallic threads. However, I prefer and use mostly polyester threads with a lustrous finish and ribbon metallic threads, such as Superior™ Glitter, a thread that gives me wonderful results with little breakage.

17

Fabric

An artist who paints with brushes and oil or watercolor paint has a vast array of colors from which to choose. As a visual artist using fiber as a medium, your fabric stash is your palette. Perhaps thinking of fabric as a color palette is a new idea to you. Keep this concept in mind when looking for fabrics during your next trip to the quilt shop. Quiltmakers are fortunate indeed. Not only can we obtain fabrics in an exciting rainbow of colors, but working with fabrics gives quiltmakers the added advantage of having color combinations of several hues, designs, patterns and textures integrated in our palette. Cutting up patches of different fabrics and mixing the colors and elements can produce many happy surprises in your quilt. You can obtain interesting results that would not be probable if you were painting the same subject with paints and a brush.

The majority of fabrics I use for my quilts are batiks and hand-dyed fabrics. When buying fabric, I look for the following:

- contrast within the piece of fabric—contrast in value (light and dark) and in color/color combinations

- unusual or striking color combinations

• any pattern or design in the fabric that is asymmetrical (not a close repetitive print)

• subtle touches or splashes of additional colors within the color palette of the fabric

• complimentary color combinations such as yellow/purple or red/teal

• the darkest dark colors and the lightest pastel colors

Fabrics have color value. Value is the spectrum of a color ranging from the lightest to darkest. You need to incorporate all values—light to dark—to achieve good contrast and balance in your work. Be aware that 90-95% of the fabrics available in quilt shops have a medium value. Take a close look at the lightest to darkest value spectrum in your fabric stash. Not surprisingly, almost all of the fabric in your stash is probably medium value as well. Most likely you have more light than dark value fabrics. If a fabric has a pattern, even a subtle one, it will read somewhere on the medium scale from a medium-light to medium-dark. The darkest fabrics in your stash may not be dark enough to get optimum contrast for your quilts. Even the darkest fabrics in a quilt shop may read only as a medium dark at best when they are compared to the

dark colors that can be obtained by hand-dyeing and over-dyeing fabric. Over-dyed fabrics are dyed a second or third time with black or another deep color. The deepest dark colors are difficult to find in commercial fabrics and many shops do not carry a good variety. I love the multicolored fabrics that are over-dyed because the colors peek through the dark and create exciting results. I find these deepest dark-valued fabrics at quilt shows and buy them from quilters who hand-dye fabric. Make it a point to be on the lookout for beautiful fabrics in these two hard to find values—very light and very dark—and when you find them —whether commercial or dyed by hand—buy them! These fabrics are the key for great contrast when putting together colors in your quilt.

Hand-dyed fabrics cost more, but they make an exciting palette and are worth the additional expense. Every inch is unique not only in color, but also in the design lines created during the dye process. Using these dye lines as a design element helps achieve movement and unusual patterns within your quilt. Mixing and blending the colors in asymmetrical batiks and hand-dyed fabrics imparts a painterly look to the quilt.

Rather than using plain black fabric for a dark contrast in your work, consider choosing the darkest shades of green, navy, purple, red and brown that you can find. These deep colors add depth and a richness you cannot get with black. Try putting the deep colors against black and you will see that the black looks flat in comparison. The dark richness of the color provides stunning contrast for your quilt.

Buy only fabric that you love. Look for fabrics that speak to you or kindle your imagination with ideas. Don't waste money on cheap goods or choose fabric only because it is on sale. Never buy so-so fabric because you think it may work "OK" in a quilt that you are making. You will always find ways to use the fabric you really like in your quilts, but the rest will sit on your shelf taking up valuable space and costing more in the long run. Also, don't hesitate to cut up and use the fabrics you love dearly. There is always more fabric to love! It is better to let the beloved fabric live on in a quilt than languish on a closet shelf.

19

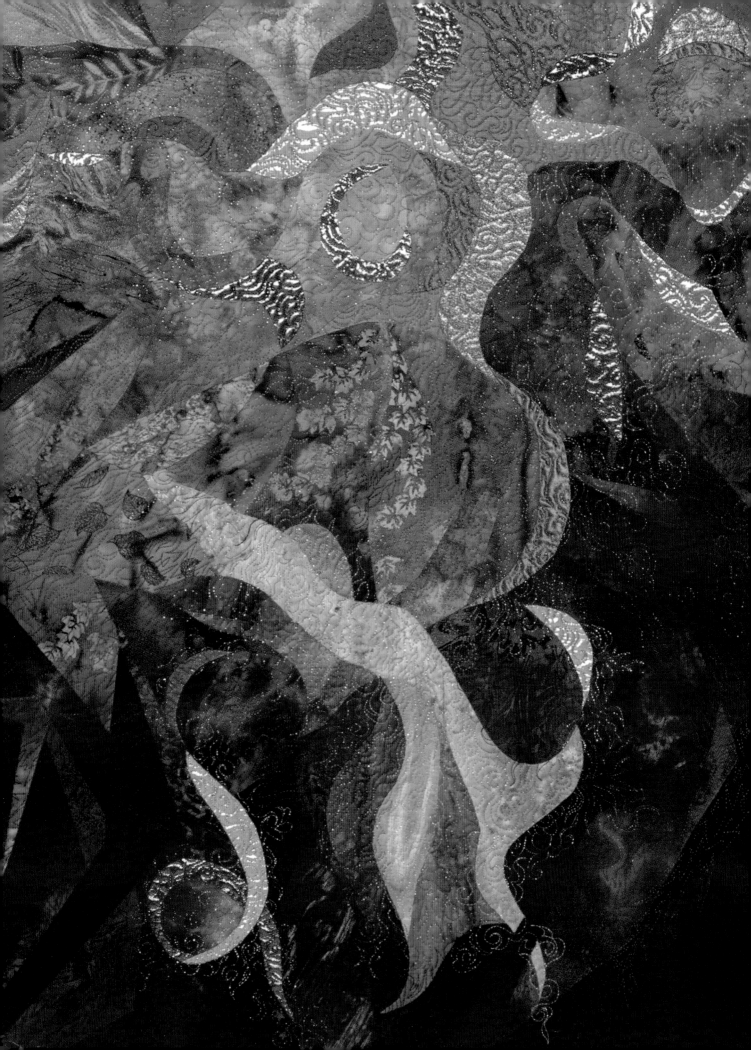

2

Color your quilt beautiful

Color is my passion. My favorite part of the quilting process is playing with color and fabrics. In this chapter I am going to offer some of my personal thoughts about color and how to use it to achieve the effects you want in all your quilting.

Left, Passages of the Spirit, *detail.*
Above, Windows.

The joy of creating a quilt, a painting or a work in any art form is having total freedom to make personal choices. One way to accomplish this is by our choice of color and fabrics. Before beginning the *My Star Dances* pattern in Chapter 3, give some thought to how your choice of color and fabrics will affect the finished quilt. Feel free to play and experiment with your project. Don't be afraid to try a new approach with the design or test unusual color combinations. Unless you leave your comfort zone—doing only what is comfortable for you—you will never grow creatively.

The elements of design

With my topstitching technique, each patch of the pattern is constructed individually on the quilt front. You have the option of using a different fabric for every patch in the design. This includes all of the background patches (called **negative space**) and all of the patches denoting the subject (called **positive space**). A design may have a single main subject or it may contain one or more contributing subjects. The **focal point** is the most important feature or center of interest in the design. You want the viewer's eyes to zero in on this area first. The focal point may be the main subject or it could be a detail within the main subject.

In *My Star Dances*, you must choose whether you want the star or the background setting to be the main subject of the design. If you choose the star, then it is the primary subject. The secondary subject is the star's tail. Besides being the main subject, the star would also be the focal point of the design. But say, for instance, that you decide to use a hand-dyed fabric for the main patch in the star. The fabric's colors and radiating dye lines give the illusion of a rift or fissure within the star. The colors emphasize the rift and catch the viewer's attention. The star is still the main subject, but now the rift detail becomes the focal point of the design. What is deemed as the main subject,

The star is still the main subject, but now the fissure detail in the body of the star becomes the focal point of the design.

contributing subjects or focal point in a design is subjective. It depends where the emphasis is placed.

Keep in mind that both the subjects (positive space) and background components are equally important in a composition. When you create a design of your own or make fabric and color choices you must give equal consideration to both components. The background is significant because its job is to develop, enhance and energize the subject. Unless you intend the background to be the focus, the background shapes, space and colors should never overpower the focal point or subjects in a composition.

My Star Dances has two elements—a simple star and the background space. Depending on the value and color choices for each element, the quilt will take on a different perspective.

The properties of color

What is value?

Value measures color on a scale from light to dark. The range of the scale is from the lightest **tint** of the color (white added) to the darkest **shade** (black added). For instance, the color violet would range in hue on the scale from the lightest tint of lavender (high value) to a shade of deepest violet (low value).

A harmonious quilt will have a balance of both light and dark colors in it, adding interest. If your quilt contains all dark hues it is somber. It has no joy or life in it. A quilt that has all tints or light colors has no depth. Dark colors need the light colors to live. Light colors need to play off the dark colors to shine.

As with all things in life, as well as art, you need a balance. Light and dark-valued colors need each other to survive. You cannot fully appreciate the light values for what they are unless you see them placed next to a dark color. Equally, unless you intersperse some light values against the dark ones, you cannot fully appreciate the dark colors.

dark

light

Value measures color on a scale from light to dark.

What is color temperature?

All colors have a **temperature**. A color can create the illusion of being warm or cold. Yellow, orange and red are warm colors. Warm colors stimulate the brain.

Blue is the ultimate cool color. Cool hues are calming and subdued. The colors of green, blue-violet and violet are combinations of blue plus a warm color. Adding yellow to blue makes green; violet is a combination of blue and red. Green and violet are considered to be cool hues but this can be subjective depending on the amount of blue versus the warm color they contain. Anytime red or yellow is added to a cool hue, such as yellow to green (yellow-green) or red to violet (reddish violet), the color takes on some degree of warmth. The larger the pro-

portion of warm hue added, the warmer the color reads.

When there is an intermingling of warm and cool colors, the eye sees warm colors first. They give the illusion of advancing and pop to the foreground. Because of this illusion warm colors are most often used for the positive space or focal point. Conversely, cool colors retreat, especially dark cool colors. They are usually chosen for the background, enhancing the subject.

Color temperature plays a role in the quilt. If you choose to make a monochromatic quilt (hues of one color) that contains only different hues of blue, the final effect will be quiet at best, and perhaps even cold, sad, or boring, depending on the hues of blue you choose. However, if you counterbalance the blue with just a dab of a warm color, such as an orange hue, it will add interest to the quilt. It doesn't take much of the warm color—just a light touch here and there. This way you keep not only the original flavor of the blue

The monochromatic blue quilt is pretty, but look how it perks up with just a few sparks of orange! Quilt surface designed by Rhonda Pfahler.

quilt, but add a warm spark of excitement to the work.

On the other hand, if you make a quilt that contains all warm hues, the resulting edgy sensations may over-stimulate, incite or even anger the viewer. Blending a few bits of a cool color into the mix will be a welcome and soothing note.

What color should I use for my star?

If you choose a warm bright color for the star, such as yellow, orange, red, etc., and cool colors for the background, such as dark blue or violet, the warm and bright colors register in the brain before dark cool colors. The star leaps forward to become the prominent element in the design, making it the main subject or focal point of the composition.

If you choose the opposite colors for your project...a dark, cool color for the star and a warm or light-colored background, you will achieve an entirely different effect. Now the star recedes into the background and it's the warm background we see first. The background becomes the point of interest or focus. Both scenarios produce valid but different outcomes. It all depends on the look and perspective you want to convey for your quilt.

Should my star shine bright?

Intensity, also called **chroma**, is the purity and strength of a color. Pure hues are the brightest colors on the color spectrum and have the most strength visually. These hues have a strong chroma. Pure hues vary in value (light to dark) as well. On the color wheel, pure yellow would have the lightest (highest) value and pure violet would have the darkest (lowest) value.

Pure hues vary in value: On the color wheel, yellow is the lightest value and violet is the darkest. They have strong chroma.

Two complementary colors mixed together will produce gray with a weak chroma.

A pure color mixed with white and black (gray) becomes a tone.

Every one of the infinite hues in the spectrum has a strong chroma before it is mixed with another color. Once you mix a pure color with white, black, gray, its complement, or any other color, you dilute the integrity of the color and it loses its intensity and strength. Its chroma weakens.

If you mix two pure hues together that are similar or adjacent on the artist's color wheel the resultant color, although diluted and slightly weaker in intensity, will still be strong. However if you mix a color with its complement or opposite on the color wheel, the mixed colors neutralize to form gray and a weak chroma.

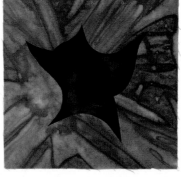

Left: the warm-colored star is the main focus. Right: the dark star recedes. The warm background catches the eye first and the background becomes the focus of the scene.

24

If you add white to a pure color, it becomes a **tint**. If you add black to a color, it become a **shade**. If you add gray, it becomes a **tone**. The vast majority of the fabrics in a quilt shop are toned colors. They are colors with gray added. There are few fabrics that are pure colors in the quilt shops. Herein lies the problem: most of what we have in our stash are toned fabrics of medium value.

To create a harmonious quilt, you should balance the intensity of the colors used. To use all toned fabrics will result in a dull quilt because the fabrics contain a lot of gray. You need to throw into the mix some bright or pure color to give it life. Vice versa, using all bright colors will make your eyes bounce off the wall. Their beauty is lost because they are competing against one another. You need to add some subdued tones to the quilt to lessen the jarring impact and give your eyes some rest. The beautiful bright colors sparkle the brightest when they are next to the toned or dull colors.

Pure colors are vibrant and strong. An intense or pure color will stand out from all the others. As an artist, you want to capture the viewers' attention and direct their eyes first to the subject matter of your quilt. Because intense colors grab the eye, they are most frequently used in the focal point area. Because intense colors are so vibrant, you should balance out pure color with tints, tones and shades.

Can I make my star glow?

Luminosity is a fun effect to experiment with. If an object is luminous, it has the appearance of emitting light or being illuminated from within. You can give your star the appearance of gleaming or radiant light by manipulating the intensity (pureness or chroma) and the texture of the fabrics you choose.

To obtain the illusion of luminosity, the background color should be of a low value (a medium dark but never black) and be heavily toned with gray (weak chroma or intensity). The focal point (star) color must be lighter in value and purer in intensity (strong chroma) than the background color or whatever is surrounding it. To achieve a luminous effect it is more important to work with contrast of intensity than of value. For the best results, use fabrics without texture and little or no printed pattern design for the object to look illuminated in the scene.

To be luminous, a color must be lighter in value and purer in intensity (strong chroma) than the background color or whatever is surrounding it.

25

Color schemes & combinations

Complementary colors

The color combinations I love using are **complementary colors**. They are hues that lie opposite one another on the color wheel. Some complementary color combinations are red-orange with blue-green, yellow with violet, red with green, orange with blue, red-violet with yellow-green and yellow-orange with blue-violet. I've found from experience that I don't have to choose colors exactly across the color wheel to achieve good results. Close seems to work as long as the colors are in the opposite vicinity.

One of the reasons I love to use complementary color combinations is because they are bold and dynamic. These colors are a natural opposite balance. Pure (intense) complementary colors enjoy the most contrast possible between colors. These colors sizzle—even pulsate—when placed next to each other.

26

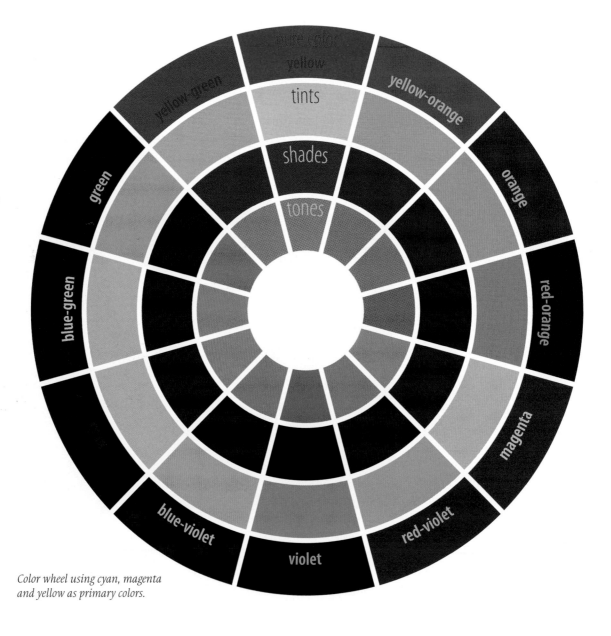

Color wheel using cyan, magenta and yellow as primary colors.

Examples of complementary colors.

The most vibrant combination of contrasting colors is pure yellow (which has the lightest value of all colors) and pure violet (which is the deepest value of all colors). When these two colors are used together they have the highest amount of contrast in both color and value. This combination will catch a viewer's eye more than any other combination. The remaining color combinations are listed in descending order of color value difference and impact:

- yellow-orange/blue-violet
- yellow-green/red-violet
- orange/blue
- red-orange/blue-green
- red/green.

At their purest (strong chroma), contrasting hues emit a startling or jarring visual impact when they neighbor and should be used sparingly or in small increments. Still, you can achieve a beautiful combination by surrounding a pure color with its complement in a diffused form—such as tints, tones or shades. For instance, pure red-orange can be tempered with a toned teal for a stunning color combination. You can also mix or match diluted complementary hues such as pale coral tint with a deep shade of teal or a toned red-orange with aqua.

Split-complementary

With a complementary scheme, a color is paired with its direct opposite across the color wheel. In a **split-complementary** scheme a color is paired with either one or both of the two colors that lie on either side of its opposite on the artist's color wheel. For instance, in a complementary scheme you could pair orange and blue. In a double split-complementary scheme you would use orange with both blue-green and blue-violet. In a single split-complementary scheme, orange would be used with either the blue-green or the blue-violet.

As with direct complementary schemes you can mix shades, tones, tints and pure colors.

An orange tint, a blue-green tone and a blue-violet shade are split-complementary colors.

Analogous colors

Analogous hues lie next to each other on the color wheel. You can use three, four or even five adjacent colors. An example of an analogous color scheme is yellow, yellow-green and green. Another would be blue, violet-blue, violet and red-violet. Rather than having a contrasting effect like complementary colors, they lend a delicate and subtle appearance to the quilt. Analogous color schemes also tend to suggest a mood or feeling, probably because of the

emphasis on color temperature. The schemes are usually restricted to either warm or cool colors. My quilt *The Promise of Spring* is based on an analogous color scheme and conveys a tranquil mood.

As with complementary colors you can mix pure hues with tints, shades and tones in an analogous scheme. Even when I use analogous colors, I throw in tidbits of a complementary color here and there. I feel it benefits the overall look by balancing both the color and temperature.

Triad and tetrad color schemes

A **triadic** scheme contains three colors that are equally spaced around the artist's color wheel in a triangle. Thus yellow is matched with red and blue. Another triad combination is green, orange and violet. A third is red-orange, yellow-green and blue-violet.

Tetrad combinations include colors that are three steps away from each other on the color wheel (a wheel with 12 colors). Red-orange, yellow, blue-green and violet is one combination. Yellow-green, blue, red-violet, and orange is another. The last is green, blue-violet, red and yellow-orange. Basically, a tetrad is a combination of two equally spaced sets of complementary colors.

Complementary, split-complementary, analogous, tetrad and triadic color schemes are all valid choices and one scheme is not better or preferable to another. The color combinations and scheme you choose in your work depend on your personal preference, taste and adherence to the look or mood you are trying to convey. In much of my work I combine all colors. It's my personal opinion that all colors go together and can be combined in any combination as long as they are balanced in value, temperature, intensity and space.

Detail, **The Promise of Spring,** *showing analogous colors.*

The look of stars

Give some thought to the effect you want to achieve with *My Star Dances*. Consider first the fabrics you want to use for the subject. In this case let's choose the star as the main focus or subject of the pattern. Because we want it to be prominent in the pattern, we will choose a warm, bright color for the star and a cool, dark color for the background. The use of cool background colors will set off the focal point.

The star in this design has two halves. The color or colors you opt to use in each half of the star will play a part in defining its configuration. If you choose the same color for both halves, both patches will "read" as one to the eye and the star will appear to be a single-shaped entity in the quilt.

If you make each half of the star a markedly different value of the same or similar colors, the star creates an illusion of being a three-dimensional object. It also elicits more interest than an object that is all one color. If you decide to use different values for your star, make sure the contrast between the two halves is strong enough to show the perspective and depth you are trying to achieve. Pin the fabrics you are considering for the star to your design wall and view them from a distance of at least ten feet to see if there is enough color contrast. Without sufficient contrast, the star will read as the same color and lose its punch.

Besides color choices, you also have to decide where to put each color in the star. Again, where you place the color determines the configuration of the star. The template numbers for the star are 2 and 6. Template 6 is the larger patch. You may construct this template with a light value fabric and Template 2 with a darker value or vice versa. Either option gives a different look to your star...it all depends on what you like.

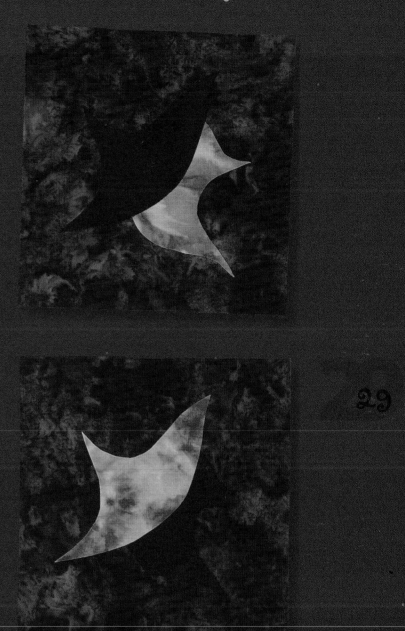

Color placement within an element makes a subtle difference.

29

Shading & highlights

Shading

You can give your star a three-dimensional look in several ways. You may use a dark-colored fabric for one patch and a lighter color of the same hue for the other. You also can heighten the impression of dimension and give your project a more realistic and painted look by the use of area shading. Although you may certainly use real fabric paints to achieve results, I do not. I love to incorporate and play with the contrast and color variations that already exist within a fabric to pull off the result I'm looking for.

If you shade the darker patch at the specific area where the lighter patch overlaps it ... intimating the lighter patch is casting a shadow, it gives an illusion of depth to the star. If you choose a fabric for the darker patch that contains not only the dark contrasting color you need to use for the shadow, but also some of the lighter color of the light patch, the painted look is heightened even more.

A shadow is usually a darker, grayer version of the same color as the object creating the shade. A good rule of thumb to follow when choosing colors to shade an object is: the shadow color should be a slightly darker hue and slightly darker or weaker in intensity than the original color of the star. Thus a shadow of red would have a purplish hue, yellow would have a greenish hue, and green would have a bluish hue. In all cases the shadow color would have a weaker intensity...that is, more gray or black in it.

Distinguish the color properties of the object that is casting the shadow. What are the color properties (intensity, hue and value) of the star fabric? Once you've determined the properties, refer to your color wheel and find the color of your star. Suppose your star is pure orange. Now drop down one color darker (toward violet) on the color wheel. Orange-red is the hue that is one step down on the color wheel. Now choose a color to shade your star within the orange-red color group that is a bit more shaded or toned (having more gray or black) than the color of your star. A shadow is always slightly darker or weaker in color intensity than the original color of the object. The hue you would use for your star's shadow should be a toned or lightly shaded reddish-orange. If your star were a toned orange instead of pure orange, you would still work within the red-orange colors, choosing a deeper toned reddish-orange or a red-orange shade. If your star were a pale orange tint, you would choose a light value tone of reddish-orange (with a weaker intensity) for the shadow.

As one who loves to bend the rules and take artistic license, I do not always practice this accepted technique for choosing a shading color. Often I will use a hue of a complementary color, or even a lighter hue of the background color, as the shading for the element in my quilt.

Highlights

Adding highlights to your work adds realism and dimension. A **highlight** is the illusion of a bright light hitting an area of color, reflecting and intensifying it. A highlight is a lighter, purer version of a color.

As with choosing a shadow color, you can reverse the theory and choose a color for the highlight. Determine the color of your object and climb one color lighter (or higher) on the color wheel toward yellow. Within that color group, choose a color that is slightly lighter and stronger in intensity.

Thus if your star is a toned orange, you would choose a lighter, more intense yellow-orange color to use as a highlight. If your star were light yellow, then you would choose a very pale tint of yellow containing lots of white. If your star is maroon, then the highlight would be a medium, slightly toned orange-red. One rule to remember is not to use a tint as a highlight for a pure color. It gives an unnatural look. You need to choose a lighter, purer version of the color instead. In the case of pure orange, choose a pure yellow-orange as the highlight color.

Right: Shading stars to achieve dimension. **Creation of the Sun and Stars,** *detail.*

Blending

Blending colors for movement

You can use a process of color blending to obtain movement in your quilt, changing from one color to another as well as moving from one value to another.

If you place two fabrics with similar colors next to each other, the human eye tends to read them as one from a distance. Even if the similar colors vary slightly in value—that is, lighter or darker—the colors flow together and the eye perceives them as a single fabric. This premise works to a limited degree with solid colors, but you can obtain amazing results using this technique with batiks and hand-dyes. It is akin to blending paints and fun to do, not only in the focal areas, but especially when working on quilt backgrounds.

You can change from one color to another by simply noting and arranging the desired color placement on the freezer paper template, then placing the template to correspond to the colors on the fabric before you cut out the patch.

Let assume your current background in progress is violet with some green interspersed. You want to introduce or switch over to a tint of burnt sienna in the next background patch. You own a beautiful batik or hand-dyed fabric that contains both the perfect color of sienna and a similar violet although it is not the same shade. You can use this fabric as

a transition fabric to make the switch from violet to sienna. Before cutting out the next template, first pencil in the notation "violet" on the freezer paper in the area where the violet is already in place. You need to carry some amount of violet through to the new patch. Make the notes close to the seam lines where the new patch joins the patch already sewn or pinned down. On the same paper template, mark "sienna" where you want to introduce the new color.

Mark "violet" where you need to carry through the existing color. Also mark where you want the new color.

When you position the freezer paper template on the transition fabric, arrange it in such a way that the colors play out the way you want them to. Look at the fabric to find an area where both the violet and tint of burnt sienna colors are close to each other. Place the "violet" portion of the template on a violet area of the fabric and match the "sienna" marking with the sienna in the fabric. Press the template in this position to the fabric and cut out.

Once the patch is pinned in place, the colors will correspond correctly in their placement and the violets will successfully blend so the change is imperceptible from a distance.

Arrange the freezer paper template on the fabric, matching the markings on the template with the colors in the fabric.

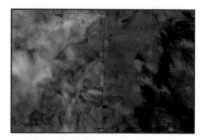

After stitching, the transition is complete and the color blending is perfect!

For the next background template, you can use either a fabric that is exclusively sienna, completing the transition to a single color, or you can choose another batik that is mostly sienna, but perhaps with a hint of some violet running through it. To change value, choose fabrics with the same or similar colors, but of a lighter value overall. Again, place similar colors together at the seams.

32

Color balance

Balance in all things

Achieving balance is a necessary requirement for a successful quilt. **Balance** is a condition where contrasting energies (such as color, chroma, temperature) or aspects (value, scale, print) counter each other and equal out, reaching an even and stable state. Most quilts are better artistically when they are balanced. The exception might be if you knowingly and deliberately use the extreme imbalance to make a specific statement on a passionate issue.

To be harmonious, color should be balanced in several aspects: hue (color vs. color), temperature (warm/cool), intensity (bright/dull), value (light/dark) and the spacing intervals or arrangement of hue. Additionally, for artistic interest the size, shape and mass of the patches should vary within the design.

Keep in mind that with color, all properties are subjective. How the relative temperature, value, intensity, etc. of a color reads will vary depending on its placement among other colors in the quilt. A red-orange hue appears to be redder when it is positioned next to a yellow patch, but the orange cast will be more apparent when it lies next to a true red. A color that reads as a dark when placed against one color may read as a light when it lies next to another color.

Arrangements for color balance

An important factor in working with colors is balancing their location or placement in the quilt. Depending on your own personal artistic style and preference, you can equalize areas of a color in a pleasing arrangement around the whole surface of the quilt. Balance can be achieved by incorporating or spacing areas of the same hue or similar color in an orderly or pleasing symmetrical arrangement on the face of the quilt surface. The size of the color area, the intensity of the color or the spacing of the color does not need to be in exact or equal increments. Interspersing a color at several proportionate locations or points throughout the quilt top creates equilibrium for the eyes as they travel around the surface of the work.

When constructing a quilt and working with color placement, I find it helpful to jot notations on the master design indicating areas where I might want to incorporate the same color as the quilt progresses. Then, as I work, the notes remind me where I intended to use the hue or a similar color for optimum balance.

Another form of color balance is by modestly echoing color in a quilt top. Echoing, a form of repetition or rhythm, is a common element in music. It can be effective in art as well by unifying or tying together the elements of the composition. You can echo colors by using fabrics for each element (background and subject) in the composition that have areas or traces of color that are present in the opposite element, thus incorporating a hint of background color into the subject

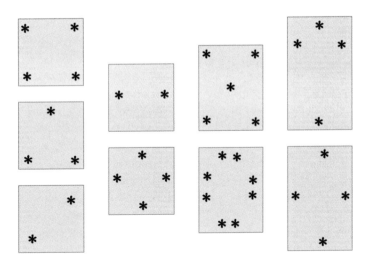

These are some spacing arrangements to help you achieve color balance.

and some of the subject color into the background. This method is my preference and style. It gives a painted look to the quilt. I love to use fabrics for the background patches that contain traces or unobtrusive small areas of subject colors. In the same way, I like to slip fabrics with a hint of background color into the subject. If this is not possible it may be done with thread color in quilting.

Echoing small amounts of color in both background and subjects is an excellent way to achieve color balance and a painterly look to your quilts. **Creation of the Sun and Stars**, *detail.*

Echoing and color balance: background vs. focal point

The secret for successful use of color is to maintain a healthy balance and contrast on many levels. One way is to distinguish between the parts or components of the design so that when a person views your work, he or she will know definitely what is the background and what is the subject. So it is with *My Star Dances*. You must choose fabrics that clearly contrast and indicate which patches denote the star and which patches represent background.

If you are echoing color in your quilt, choose fabrics for the background that contain small dabs or nuances of the subject or focal point color. However, do not incorporate so much of the color that the background becomes muddled or that the viewer's eye is confused as to where the subject, in this case the star, ends and the background begins. A little bit or trace of color goes a long way.

You must be careful that you do not incorporate too much of the background color in the star as well or it will lose its identity. Even though each element....the subject and the background.... contains some of the opposite's colors, the viewer must be able to differentiate between them easily.

Do not use a warm-colored piece of fabric that is or appears to be a solid color for a background patch where a star is not intended. You must be careful as well when constructing a background patch from fabric that contains a large amount of warm or bright color. The warm color will pop forward, causing the background patch to compete and read as part of the star or focal point.

Warm, out of place colors in the background confuse the viewer and dilute the effect you are trying to achieve. This is true even if the warm color you use in the background is different from the one used in the focal point.

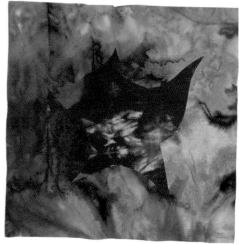

Too much warm color in the background will cause confusion.

Contrast

What is contrast?

In quilting, **contrast** is the marked distinction between colors, hues, values, intensity and temperature. Contrast sets apart and defines the elements in a composition. For example, without sufficient contrast, you would not be able to distinguish the subject from the background nor define the details in the subject such as form, shape or shading.

To use color effectively and create the best look for your quilt, you need to include contrast and balance of **color, value, print** (busy and quiet fabrics), **scale** (size of print), **temperature** and **intensity** or **chroma**.

Why contrast is important

In real life and especially bright daylight, most of us can view, perceive and judge subtle differences such as the multiple colors of yellow in the petals of a sunflower. But in artwork and on a two-dimensional surface like an artist's canvas—which is essentially what your quilt top is—you do not have that luxury. Subtle colors placed next to each other wash out and the quilt loses visual impact.

If you are making a flower in your quilt and use fabrics for the petals that are too similar in color and value, you won't see separate petals. The fabrics will blend together and the flower will read as single

blob or mass of color when you stand away from your work. While blending colors may be desirable when working with the background patches, it's imperative to define the form and shape of a focal point element—in this case the flower petals.

To create the same illusion of color that exists in the real life sunflower, you'll need to exaggerate the contrasts (e.g. value, color, etc.) to achieve the defining look needed for the quilt by using fewer and distinctly different colors of yellow to identify and separate the petals from one another.

Summer's Bounty, *detail. A real sunflower does not have all these hues of yellow and gold in the petals but in art, you must exaggerate the contrast to achieve distinction.*

It is important to distinguish not only the elements within the subject, in this case the flower petals, but also between the elements of the design—the subject and the background. If the colors in the focal point are too similar in color and value to those of the background, the impact is lost and it is not clear where one element (subject or background) stops and another begins. The focal point is diminished. Your focal point should always stand out from the background and be the most prominent feature in terms of size, color, intensity, space and value in the quilt. This effect is achieved by using contrast.

36

Since the human eye tends to read printed fabrics with similar colors as one from a distance and perceive them as one, it is important to make sure there is sufficient contrast in this area as well. If you use fabrics with similar values or fabrics with little variation in the print or pattern design—and this includes batiks—the eye becomes confused, seeing only the busyness of the fabric. It doesn't know what to look at first or how to read what it sees. Your fabrics register as a mishmash. As your eye travels over the quilt, it needs areas to rest before moving on. This is accomplished by using some quiet fabrics—ones with little or no print or pattern—to create a refuge for the eyes.

Contrast, like color, needs to be balanced. Too little contrast and the quilt is monotonous and dull. Contrast that is too sharp may have a jarring effect on the eyes and hurt or slow the flow of the design because the eye does not move easily across the quilt.

Viewing color contrast and balance from a distance

From my many years of teaching I find the most challenging step most quilters face is choosing fabrics for a quilt. The lack of balance and contrasts within the quilt and between the colors of fabrics used is probably the number one misstep in quilting. One way to be sure you have enough contrast is to step back and view your choices of fabric from a distance. I can't stress this step strongly enough! You will be amazed when you start viewing fabrics from a distance. What seems to be a good contrast between two colors 12-inches from your eyes may wash out, totally disappear or read as the same color when viewed from a distance of ten feet.

You should always view your fabric color choices this way for best results. When I am in the process of constructing a quilt top, I audition every fabric before I cut and put it in my quilt. I attach the quilt top in progress to my design board with straight pins. Then I pin the fabric in question next to the patches I've already completed

and step back to see if there is adequate contrast between them before I cut out the patch.

Capricious color

Color is fleeting. Light is what enables us to see color. Without light, there is no color, only blackness. Not only does color change continuously during daylight hours but it changes subtly with the seasons as well. Artificial lighting—whether incandescent (yellow), tungsten (orange), fluorescent (greenish-blue) or full spectrum—gives a different cast to a color. Even daylight can have a red, yellow or blue cast depending on the position of the sun. Just be aware that the colors you choose to put together in a room lighted by an incandescent light bulb may appear totally different when viewed in daylight or a different type of artificial light.

Daylight provides the best advantage for choosing colors. For me the best time to choose fabric color is in the morning and early afternoon hours. I have difficulty interpreting color successfully in the evening even though my workroom is equipped with full-spectrum lighting.

The background opportunities

Consider your options for choosing background colors in your quilt. Because each patch is constructed separately you don't have to use the same fabric for all the background patches...now you have the freedom to create unusual effects with color for your project. Perhaps you would like to gradate the color in the background patches by arranging the colors in a series of levels or steps in such a way that the color changes gradually from one step to the next without being too obvious. You can gradate color according to value (light to dark), intensity (brightness) or hue (changing from one color to another). You may choose to change the value of a color in your background in several different ways.

Opt for one of these suggestions or select any arrangement of colors and placement for the background that pleases you. As a child (and still as an adult) I loved to daydream when gazing at the clouds and envision ethereal animal shapes and other objects floating in the sky. In the same way, stretch your imagination as you look at the shapes of the background patches in the pattern. Will two or more adjoining shapes combine to create an interesting flowing design? See if you can envision unique or creative ways to arrange colors for your quilt's background.

*Change the background for interesting effects. In **Sunflower**, the swath of lighter value fabric runs on the diagonal.*

37

Passages of the Spirit

QUILTING BY IMPROVISATION

Taking artistic license

Too often we visualize and use color only in a realistic context. We make skies blue and flowers red. But as artists, we are not bound by convention or realism. Rather than being a slave to tradition, we can create our own world and color it with unusual choices. Why must the sky always be blue? At one time or another I've seen the sky in every color—even a sickly yellowish green.

What about trees? The leaves can be every color from yellow to violet. Green is only one choice of many for leaf color. Color for tree trunks does not have to be the traditional brown. Choices for the tree trunk can contain a gamut of colors—anywhere from the deepest navy, reds, greens and violets to using light-toned oranges and pinks as bark highlights.

We should always consider unique approaches and different viewpoints with design and color choices. It is the unique that catches our attention, not the mundane. Thus, red skies or blue trees are more interesting to view because they are exceptional and not the norm.

My last word about color...

In this chapter I've given you a lot to think about. I've explained some basic concepts about color and design. But you must remember that rules in art are not hard and fast. Every rule can be broken for individuality and special effect. Just know and be aware of the effects you'll get when you break the rules. The main and only rule you must follow is to relax and not let color intimidate you. Have fun and muster the courage to experiment!

3 Crazy About Curves basic technique

Using *My Star Dances*, a pattern inspired by my quilt, *Creation of the Sun and Stars*, follow me as I guide you step by step through the construction process. You'll learn that creating curves in quilts has never been easier as you quickly master my "Crazy About Curves" technique.

Left, Creation of the Sun and Stars, *detail.*
Above, Creation of the Sun and Stars.

My Star Dances

The pattern size is 13" x 13". The finished size will vary depending how you choose to finish the pattern. For fabric, use assorted scraps and small amounts of fabric for star, background and sleeve. You will need a 17" x 17" piece of stabilizer.

On the *My Star Dances* pattern, page 168, Templates 1, 4, 5, 7 and 9 are background patches. Templates 2 and 6 are the primary star patches. Templates 3 and 8 are flames trailing from the star.

Interpreting the pattern markings

- The drawn lines are the actual seam lines.

- The **numbers** on the templates are the order of sequence for construction.

- The **small arrows** marked on the edge(s) of the freezer paper template indicate which seam allowance(s) need to be turned under.

- Align **long arrows** with fabric pattern design lines to obtain directional flow or achieve movement.

- The symbol |×× indicates a "stop turn" command. The fabric seam allowance should be turned under along the edge (with arrows) to the |×× symbol. Stop turning the fabric under at the symbol and let the crease trail off to raw edge allowance. There is no need to snip or make a cut in the fabric allowance. A successive patch will overlap and cover the remaining raw seam allowance.

- **Hash mark |** is a single line that bisects the seam line between patches. Its sole purpose is to correctly reposition a newly constructed freezer paper/patch back into the pattern.

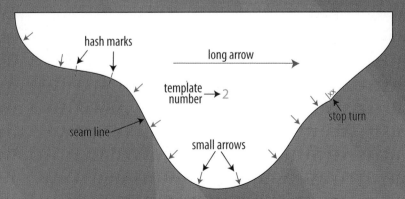

Lets begin working...

Place the *My Star Dances* master pattern face up on a table and secure the corners with tape. Tear off a section of freezer paper large enough to completely cover the pattern and place it on top of the pattern with the waxy side down. Tape the corners of the freezer paper to the table. In most cases the lines and markings are clearly visible through the freezer paper. If you have difficulty seeing the pattern markings through the freezer paper, use a light table, a glass top table with a lamp underneath or simply tape the pattern and freezer paper to a window during daylight hours.

1 Trace the pattern on the freezer paper and include all markings. Add a long directional arrow to a pattern template if you wish to add movement to a patch.

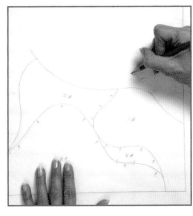

Trace all the pattern lines, markings and arrows.

2 Carefully remove the tape on both the master pattern and freezer paper and set the master pattern aside, saving it for reference. The quilt top will be constructed using only the traced pattern on the freezer paper.

3 Cut a piece of light or mid-weight stabilizer at least 2 " larger on all sides than the size of the pattern. Center the freezer paper pattern right side up on the stabilizer. Secure with ample straight pins so the pattern will not shift.

Marking a template for movement in the quilt

There may be times you would like to incorporate movement in your project. With the *My Star Dances* pattern, you can create the illusion of a shooting star by choosing fabric with swirling lines or a hand-dyed or batik fabric with a starburst pattern. You can position the background template on the fabric to take advantage of the print or dye lines to create the impression of movement.

If you decide to add movement in a background patch, draw a long arrow on the freezer paper template to indicate the direction you want the movement to flow before you cut the template out of the pattern. The arrow can be straight or curved depending on the effect you want and the print or lines of the fabric you are considering.

Mark the paper template with a long arrow to indicate the direction of flow.

4 Cut only Template 1 out of the freezer paper pattern on the traced seam line. *Do not cut the stabilizer foundation.* Leave the remainder of the freezer paper pattern intact and pinned to the foundation. Template 1 is a background patch in the *My Star Dances* pattern, so place it waxy side down on the right side of the background fabric. If you chose to add movement to this patch and drew a long directional arrow on the paper template, position the template on the fabric so the direction of the arrow aligns and corresponds with the movement or direction of the lines in the fabric.

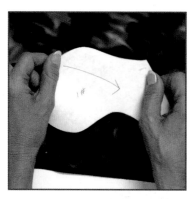

If your template has a directional arrow marked on it, align the arrow with the lines of the fabric. Press paper Template 1 to the right side of the background fabric.

5 Iron the freezer paper to the right side of the fabric using a steam iron on a cotton setting. Press well. Cut the patch out of the fabric, leaving fabric seam allowances on all sides of the paper template. Leave a generous seam allowance of ¾" to one inch on any side of a template that is an outside edge or border of the quilt. This allows room for error while adding borders, shrinkage due to quilting and fast finish procedures.

Leave seam allowances on all sides of the template.

Leave ⅜" to ⅝" for seam allowance between each patch. There is no need to measure a seam allowance; simply guesstimate. Please don't skimp on fabric for a seam allowance or cut it only ¼"! The beauty of this method is the ability to be flexible and cover up any mistakes. If you cut out patches with a generous seam allowance, you can easily adjust the extra fabric to cover errors.

6 There are no small arrows on Template 1, so you do not turn under any seam allowances. With the freezer paper side up, return the paper template/fabric to its place in the freezer paper pattern—the hole from which it was cut—aligning and matching the edges of the template with the edges of the uncut pattern. This is like putting the last piece of a jigsaw puzzle in place.

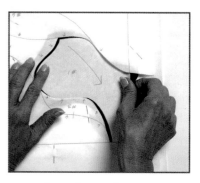

Return the patch to its place in the pattern, using the edges of the freezer paper as a guideline.

Nudge the fabric seam allowances on all sides of the template to lie beneath the surrounding freezer paper pattern. Using a straight pin to loosen the fabric at a corner of the freezer paper, gently remove it from the fabric. Pin the patch to the foundation stabilizer. Pin only the fabric to the foundation, not the freezer paper.

Note: If the freezer paper does not stick well to the fabric, the iron temperature is probably too low. Increase the heat setting. If the freezer paper shreds or does not peel away easily from the fabric, the iron is too hot. Lower the temperature setting slightly. Use a lower iron temperature and a protective piece of parchment paper or press cloth when ironing materials such as lamé and other types of fussy or delicate fabrics.

44

Lining a patch

In Step 7, Template 2 is part of the star. If you want to make your star or trailing flame a light color—such as yellow-orange—with a dark background, you may find the seam allowance of the dark fabric shadows through the light orange star fabric. Eliminate the shadowing by constructing a lining for the yellow-orange patch. Cut out the freezer paper template twice—first with a lining fabric and the second time with the patch fabric. In extreme cases cut two or more linings for the patch. The added thickness of the linings will not show, affect the stitching or detract from the look of the finished piece.

Choosing a lining fabric

You have several options for a lining fabric. You may use either a densely woven white fabric or muslin with excellent results. You may also use the same fabric as the patch. A third option, for artistic effect, is to choose a strong, deep-value patterned fabric that deliberately shows through the light-colored patch, lending depth and interest.

a) Place and press freezer paper template on the lining fabric.

b) Cut out lining patch leaving a seam allowance on all sides *except* the edges marked with an arrow.

Cut out template from the lining fabric first. Cut away the seam allowance from the edge marked with arrows, but leave a seam allowance on all other edges.

Trim fabric on marked edge on seam line. Remove the freezer paper from the patch and set aside.

c) Press the same freezer paper template to the desired patch fabric and cut out, leaving seam allowances on all sides. Construct as usual, clipping valley curves and turning under the edges marked with arrows. Press.

d) Flip the constructed template over, wrong side up. Flip over the lining. Please note that the lining needs to be reversed to fit properly. Position it on the back of the patch so the cut edge of the lining aligns and fits snugly in the crease of the patch. Tack the seam allowance of the patch intermittently to the lining with bits of fusible web to secure it so it doesn't shift.

e) Replace the patch in the pattern and resume piecing.

Tacking

As a general rule you do not tack down the turned under seam allowances on patches with this technique. However there are times when it may be necessary to secure the turned seam allowance to the back of the patch, to a piece of lining or to the stabilizer in order to hold the allowance in place until it is stitched down. I use fusible webbing on a roll to fix the allowance in place.

While holding the roll of webbing in the palm of your hand, insert the end tip of the webbing between the fabrics to be tacked together. Press the tip of the iron to the fabric area but be careful not to touch the iron to the webbing. As the webbing melts, pull away the excess still on the roll.

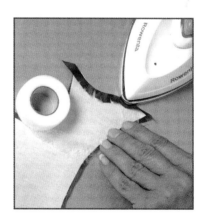

To tack a seam allowance, insert the webbing between the turned seam allowance and the back of the patch. Touch the allowance with the tip of the iron, pulling away the webbing as it melts.

7 Cut out Template 2 from the freezer paper. This piece is the top of the star. Press paper Template 2 to the desired star fabric. Cut out the patch, leaving fabric seam allowance on all sides. The seam allowance should be between ⅜" to ⅝". Note the edge of the patch with the small arrows. This is the only seam to be turned under. Most of the marked edge of Template 2 is a concave (valley) curve and must be clipped to turn under smoothly.

8 Carefully clip the seam allowance on Patch 2.

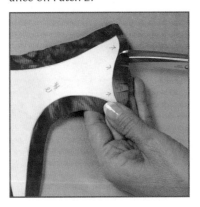

Clip and turn under only the edge or edges of a patch that are marked with small arrows.

9 Using your thumb and forefinger, begin turning the clipped seam allowance to the back of the patch, using the edge of the freezer paper as a guideline.

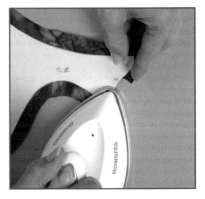

Using the edge of the freezer paper as a guide, turn under the seam allowance on the edge marked with small arrows and press.

Your goal is to achieve a smooth creased fold line with no points or clips showing. Attaining a smooth edge is more important than following the freezer paper line with obsessive precision. If some of the clips you made show on the crease/fold, press out the crease and turn under the seam allowance again, this time making the curve a little deeper until the clip cuts are no longer visible.

Note: The only seam allowance on a patch that is turned under is the edge marked with the small arrows. The remaining edges are left flat. Most patches in a pattern have only one edge marked for turning. In some cases a patch may need to have two or three sides (edges) turned. Remember, if a seam isn't marked, don't turn it under!

Clipping Curves

46

When working with curves, you will notice that there are concave and convex curves. An easy way to remember the difference is to remember them as mountains and valleys...the convex curves resemble mountains and the concave curves are valleys.

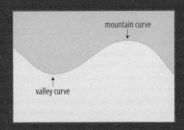

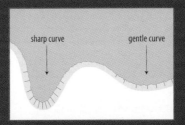

To turn under the fabric seam allowance of a valley curve smoothly, you must first clip it. Clip the fabric close to the freezer paper edge. The number and depth of clips you need to make on a patch depend on the acuteness of the curve. Gentle curves require fewer clips than sharp curves.

Clip the valley curves only on the edge(s) marked with small arrows. Do NOT clip seam allowances on edges that are unmarked. Also, never clip the allowance on a mountain curve. Clipping mountain curves produces points in the crease of the seam allowance and you will not obtain a smooth edge.

10 Return the patch to the pattern, aligning the edges of the freezer paper. Holding the patch down securely, loosen the paper and peel it off gently, pinning the creased edge of Patch 2 to Patch 1 and the stabilizer as you go.

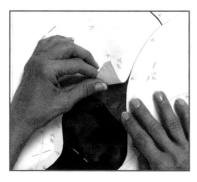

Return Patch 2 to its place in the pattern, matching freezer paper edges. Carefully remove the freezer paper as you pin the second patch to Patch 1 and the stabilizer.

11 Template 3 is a flame or extension of the star. Cut out the freezer paper template and press to fabric. The edge with the small arrows on this template contains both valley and mountain curves.

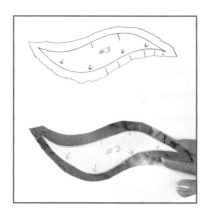

Many patches contain both mountain and valley curves. Always clip the valley curves, but never clip mountain curves.

Explorations

If points form as you turn under the seam allowance on a mountain curve, there are only two causes... either you clipped the convex curve or you still need to trim away a bit more fabric allowance. Moisten the points with a drop of water, press, and then trim allowance. Be careful not to cut off too much at once. If you do cut an allowance too short, you may reposition the freezer paper template on the fabric if there is enough room or re-cut the patch.

Clip the seam allowance on the gentle curve, but not the mountain curve. For mountain edges to be turned under evenly, first cut out the patch with a healthy allowance of ⅜" and then trim down the allowance if needed to about ¼" or so. You do not need to measure, just use your judgment. The sharper the mountain curve, the narrower the seam allowance fabric will need to be trimmed. Cut off a little bit of fabric at a time—just enough to get a smooth crease without points when you turn under the allowance. Remember—do not clip allowances on mountain curves! Once the patch is completed, return it to its place in the pattern and pin in place. If either end tip of the patch protrudes beyond the freezer paper pattern, simply fold the tail beneath itself and pin it in place.

12 Repeat these steps to construct Template 4. Keep in mind that Patch 4 has a stop turn (| xx) marking. Once you pass the marking, allow the folded allowance to fade to raw edge. After you construct and pin four or five patches in place in a pattern, it's time to sew them down.

After the patches are sewn in place, press well before you resume constructing the remaining patches. As you finish constructing the remaining templates, keep in mind that Patch 7 has a stop turn marking. Also, both end tips on Patch 8, the tiny flame, will extend beyond the paper pattern. Fold these protruding tips under so they lie beneath the patch and secure them with a straight pin.

Stitching

Once you construct four or five patches in the pattern you may begin the stitching process. When working on other patterns having many templates, work with sets of four to six patches, constructing and stitching as described before continuing with the next set of patches. When working with more than one set of patches, do not remove the uncut freezer paper pattern from the quilt top/stabilizer when you sew. Leave it pinned securely in place. Simply jelly roll the edges of the quilt top as needed until it fits under the machine. Don't worry if the freezer paper becomes crinkled; it will smooth out when you begin piecing again.

To begin stitching, decide what type of stitch you prefer. For an invisible look finish, choose a machine blind hemstitch. Another option is to use a small blanket stitch. You may consider using a large blanket stitch for a folk art look or any pretty decorative stitch available on your machine.

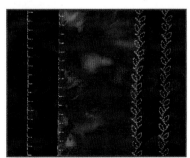

You may use blanket (left) or decorative stitches (right) as well as the blind hemstitch.

Depending on the effect you want, you may use a matching or blending thread to stitch down the patches on your quilt top for least visibility, or you may choose contrasting thread color or even decorative or metallic threads.

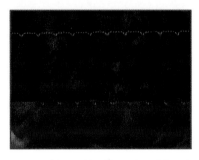

Use matching or blending color of thread for least visible stitches.

To sew the seam with the blind hemstitch, place the needle so the straight stitches in the blind hemstitch lie on the bottom patch, but the bite (∧) of the blind hemstitch reaches over to catch the overlapping patch. The distance between bites should be approximately ⅜". Position the needle to stitch in the ditch and drop precisely next to the crease (the turned under seam allowance) of the overlapping patch.

Position the needle to stitch in the ditch. The bite must catch the overlapping template.

For the least visible stitches, use a thread color that matches or blends with the color of the overlapping patch.

Start stitching down the seam by either locking the thread in place with a forward/back/forward stitch or by lifting the edge of a successive patch that overlaps the patch you are stitching down, stitching beneath it, then re-pinning the overlapping patch back in place after you stitch. End the stitching process in the same manner. Always start stitching a new seam in a direction away from a seam already stitched in place...never moving toward it. If you sew toward a seam already locked in place, chances are good the patch you are stitching will stretch and create a pucker or pleat where it meets the locked seam.

Sew the patches down in the same numerical sequence that you pieced them. That way, if a fabric patch stretches during stitching, you will be able to unpin an overlapping patch and smooth the stretched fabric beneath it, thus hiding the excess material...in effect, sweeping it under the rug without anyone being the wiser! Then replace the overlapping template, re-pin and resume stitching in sequence.

Hint: After sewing down a seam, cut the top thread before pulling the fabric away. The bobbin automatically pulls the top thread to the back of the quilt top.

Turning under straight edges and corners

A patch having a straight marked edge is easy to construct. Simply turn under the seam allowance fabric along the freezer paper edge and press with the iron.

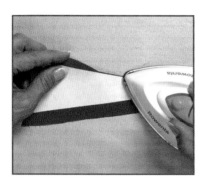

To construct straight-edged patches, simply turn under the seam allowance on the marked edge of the template.

If you must turn under the allowance on two adjoining sides of a patch, first turn under one marked side of the patch and press. Next turn under the second marked edge creating a smooth corner and press.

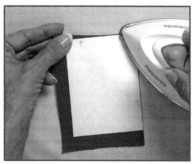

Some patches in a design may require that the seam allowances be turned under on two or more edges. To turn under the seam allowance on a corner patch, first turn under the seam allowance on edge 1, then turn under edge 2.

Corners with angles measuring 90° or more are easy to turn. If a corner is narrower than 90° and it does not look neat, first turn under the tip of the corner fabric to the back, then turn under Side 1, lastly, turn under Side 2.

To turn under the seam allowance on a mildly acute corner, first turn under the tip. Tack the tip with fusible webbing .

Turn under the seam allowance on one edge of the patch...

...and then the other edge.

49

Enlarging the stabilizer foundation

As you begin to construct medium and large quilts you'll find it necessary to enlarge the stabilizer foundation to accommodate the pattern. To increase the size of the foundation, overlap by about ¾" the adjoining (side by side) edges of two sheets of stabilizer. Fuse them with a strip of ⅝" fusible webbing to join the edges of the seam. Use a press cloth to protect the sole plate of the iron. Do not stitch the stabilizer sheets together—they will pucker.

The fusing technique to enlarge the foundation will hold up well

as you construct the patches and will not be bulky or show through the fabric. You may add stabilizer in any direction as needed for the quilt top.

To enlarge stabilizer, lay a strip of fusible webbing on the edge of one sheet of stabilizer and overlap it with the edge of the second sheet. Fuse the sheets together.

Remember:

This is a forgiving and flexible technique. You really have to work hard to make a mistake, and even those mistakes can be easily fixed. Here are a few basic rules you need to remember:

- When cutting out a freezer paper template from the pattern, do NOT cut the stabilizer foundation.

- Cut out and construct only one template at a time to retain accuracy.

- Leave seam allowances on all sides of the template.

- Turn under the seam allowance only on the edge(s) of the template marked with small arrows. Edges not marked with arrows are left flat and are not clipped.

- Do NOT clip the fabric seam allowances on mountain (convex) curves—clip only valley (concave) curves before turning the allowance under.

- Allow more than ¼" for a seam allowance.

A Quick Review

These review steps will help jog your memory as you work.

1 Place the pattern face up on a table or flat surface and cover with a sheet of freezer paper larger than the pattern. Tape the freezer paper, shiny side down, to the table.

2 Trace all lines, numbers, arrows and other markings in the pattern on the dull side of freezer paper.

3 Center and pin the freezer paper pattern to a piece of stabilizer larger than the pattern.

4 Construct the patches in numerical sequence. Begin by cutting out freezer paper Template 1 and pressing it to the right side of the appropriate fabric. Cut out the patch, leaving a seam allowance on all sides.

5 Return the patch to its place in the pattern, aligning the freezer paper edges. Loosen the paper template along the patch edges and pin the fabric to the stabilizer. Remove the paper template completely and discard.

6 Cut out paper Template 2 and press it to the right side of the fabric. Cut out the patch, leaving seam allowances on all sides. Turn under the seam allowance on the edge(s) marked with small arrows, clipping all valley curves. Press the seam allowance with an iron to set the crease. Return patch to its place in the pattern. The creased, turned seam allowance will overlap the raw edges of the previously laid patch. Pin Patch 2 in place on the stabilizer, remove the freezer paper template and discard.

7 After completing a batch of four or five patches, stitch the patches down in the same order you constructed them using a blind hemstitch with matching or blending threads. Press well.

8 Resume constructing the remaining patches in the pattern. Stitch and press.

Hints

- When you cut out a patch from fabric, leave plenty of seam allowance. This allows room to cover any mistakes you make. If you err while turning under a seam, remove the freezer paper from the patch, reposition and press it a bit lower on the fabric.

- If you have a protruding tail from a turned seam allowance, turn the tail under, tucked beneath itself, and pin. A succeeding patch will cover it.

- Be flexible. If you want to alter a patch (enlarge or subtract area) in the pattern, simply redraw or cut out the seam line as you wish. Since this is a free layering technique, there are no precise points to match. If you choose to alter the pattern by choice or by error, no one knows. Wherever two or more seams intersect, points match!

51

Congratulations! You just learned the basic concept for my topstitch technique. It will not take you long to master this fast and simple method of constructing curves. To explore border options and learn new finishing techniques for your project, refer to Chapter 7.

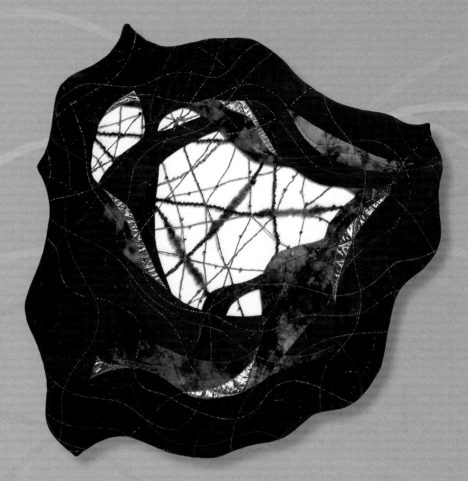

Improvisational quilts

The definition of **improvisation** is to create spontaneously with little advance thought or preparation. Improvisation in quilting represents total artistic freedom because there are no rigid patterns to follow, no points to match nor even a predetermined idea of what the quilt should look like. There are only three rules to remember in this technique. First, cover up the raw edges of a previously laid patch with another patch. Second, maintain a good value contrast between light and dark patches and the most important rule: have fun being creative!

Left, **Running in Circles***, detail.*
Above, **Dreamcatcher***. To better define the latticework, the quilt's opening is shown with a white background.*

Making an improvisational block quilt

In this chapter you will learn to use improvisation to create blocks for a quilt top. The blocks for the quilt may be constructed in many different shapes such as squares, rectangles, ovals, circles, teardrops, triangles or diamonds. You will make a series of four blocks and then join them together to make a free-form shaped quilt. Oh, one more thing—making an improvisational quilt is the perfect vehicle and a terrific way to utilize all those wonderful scraps of fabric you've been collecting for years!

Although improvisational quilts may contain as many blocks as you wish, in this chapter we will limit the number of blocks in our sample quilt to four. Each block may contain as few as three patches, up to as many as nine or more, depending on how large you want a block to be. The patches are made with a variety of fabrics and scraps chosen at random. While you may decide to make a block in a specific shape—such as a triangle—each patch within that block is cut and formed freely at will and it can be any shape you desire.

The patches in each block are sub-divided into layers or rows. A block may have either two or three distinct layers of patches. The first or bottom layer consists of a single patch and is laid down on a foundation of Pellon™ stabilizer. It is the center of the block and considered to be the first layer. Next, the raw edges of the center patch are overlapped and covered with the turned under seam allowances of the

next or second layer of patches. The number of patches comprising the second layer may vary at your discretion, but the average is about three or four patches. Once the patches in the second layer are positioned in place, pinned and sewn down, you may proceed to construct the third layer of patches. As before, the turned under seam allowances of the third layer of patches will overlap the raw edges of the second layer. Again, the number of patches needed for the third layer varies, with the average being four to six patches.

Value contrasts and color within the block

The three layers of patches in each block are constructed mainly on the basis of light vs. dark values. Attaining enough contrast in value (light vs. dark) between layers in a block is actually more important than choosing colors. All the patches within a layer should be

the same value even though the patches may vary in color. For example, every patch in the second layer of a block might be a similar light-valued tint of orange using a variety of fabrics. Or, you might choose and mix several different colors for the fabric patches in the layer, such as tints of orange, yellow and red. The colors do not matter much as long as the lightness, or value, of the fabrics are the same or similar.

While every patch within a layer is the same value, each layer of patches should be a different value than its adjoining layers. For instance, if the center patch is a dark value fabric, the next or second layer might be a light value. In turn, the patches in the third layer may be either a medium value or you could repeat the dark value since either would contrast with the light-valued second layer.

There is no specific order or sequence to follow when deciding values for the layers other than personal preference. Rather than choose a dark center patch as you did in the example above you could choose to make the center patch a light value, the second layer of patches could be a medium value and the third layer of patches in dark values. Whatever you decide, just be sure to maintain a healthy value contrast between the layers. Without a significant contrast between the layers in the block, all the fabric patches will blend together and you will see only a mishmash of colors. Without distinctly separate layers, a block has no structure, character or visual interest. Remember, color and value are subjective. Any color takes on a different cast each time it is juxtaposed to another color. The value of a fabric varies as well, depending on the value of the fabric you compare it with. A fabric considered as the dark value in one quilt block may be the light value in another. It may help to separate your fabrics and scraps into light, medium and dark values before you begin. I strongly recommend you use a design board for this project. View potential fabric choices from a distance and audition them for sufficient contrast before you cut out patches and use them in your block.

Idylls of Summer

Choosing fabrics

You may incorporate many different and unusual fabrics in your block, including cotton, silk and metallic lamé. For this project it is fun to work with a theme. You may choose a summer garden theme and incorporate fabrics with flowers, butterflies, bees and sky. Other themes might be weather, destinations such as the beach, desert or tropics, or holidays. Consider using a collage of fabrics you collected while traveling on a special vacation. These simple quilts make great gifts. They go together quickly and you can personalize the quilt for your friend or relative by choosing his/her favorite theme or special interest and using the appropriate fabrics.

Remember that printed fabrics, such as the themed fabrics mentioned above, will probably be a medium or medium-dark value. Be aware of this fact when you use these specialty fabrics and you are considering the value contrasts and order of the layers in your block. Plan accordingly. If the themed or printed fabrics are medium values, choose fabrics for the adjoining layers in the block that are distinctly light or dark values so you see a visual contrast. Also, remember to balance the busyness of printed fabrics

For the Love of Thais, *detail. The woman for whom this quilt was made is a barrel racer in rodeos.*

by incorporating some quiet fabrics in the other layers in the block. Without competition from too many other printed fabrics, the themed fabrics will become more prominent and the overall effect less confusing for the viewer. Keep in mind as you use themed or printed fabrics that you can form and cut the shape of the patch around a specific or random motif, such as a bird, butterfly or other interesting pattern in the fabric, and position the motif so it is prominent in the block.

As a first step, determine a color scheme for your quilt. You may choose to limit the colors in the quilt to only a few or you may decide to work with many colors.

Rosemary's Garden, *detail. In the collection of Rosemary and Ray Conaway.*

56

Here are some options:

- Mix different colors of patches in a block at random, with your only concern being value changes.

- Use a variation of the same or similar color in every block. For instance, you might place a red patch, a blue patch and a violet patch in each of the four blocks in a quilt.

- Construct most of the patches in a block from fabrics that have similar colors but different values. For example, the patches in a block might be pink, red and maroon.

- Construct a block in similar colors as above, but make each block in the quilt a different color. For example, one block might contain mostly blue fabrics, another block mostly reds, and so forth. Once the blocks are joined together they form a multi-color quilt. My quilt, *Running In Circles* is an example of making most of the patches in each block a specific color.

You will construct the blocks one at a time for our sample improvisational quilt. Just as with my topstitch appliqué technique, fabric patches are cut out randomly without regard to grain. A stabilizer foundation supports each block and prevents it from stretching out of shape, especially when arranging the blocks into a final shape for the quilt top and during the sandwiching and quilting processes. The foundation for the individual blocks should be lighter in weight than the Pellon™ stabilizer normally used as foundation. If possible, I suggest you use a small piece of lightweight stabilizer as the foundation for each separate block. After all the blocks are constructed they are arranged and stitched to a large, heavier sheet of Pellon™ stabilizer to form the quilt top. If you have difficulty finding stabilizer in different weights, don't stress, simply use what you have.

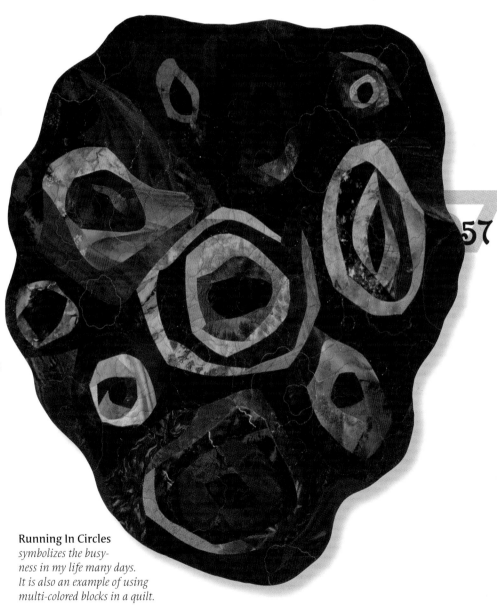

Running In Circles
*symbolizes the busy-
ness in my life many days.
It is also an example of using
multi-colored blocks in a quilt.*

Constructing a freeform basic block

First or bottom layer

As a teaching example we will create a free-form square block with a dark center, a second layer of medium-value patches and a third layer of patches that repeat the dark value. If you substitute light-valued patches for one of the layers and need to line a patch, please refer to page 63.

Cut and press a piece of light-weight stabilizer approximately 14" x 14". Lay it down on a flat surface. For Patch 1 cut out a piece of dark fabric or use a suitable scrap that measures approximately 4"x 5". It does not matter what shape the patch is. The patch can be any irregular four-sided shape or it may resemble an oval or even be triangular in shape. Press the fabric patch smooth. Center Patch 1, right side up, on the stabilizer. Secure the patch to the stabilizer with a single straight pin placed in the center of the patch.

Center patch 1, right side up, on the stabilizer.

Second layer

Your objective now is to cover the raw edges of the dark center patch with a second layer of fabric patches in an interesting arrangement of shapes. Use either three or four patches for the second layer. If you select three patches you'll end up with a triangular shaped block; using four patches will give an asymmetrical, boxy look to the block. Choose a medium value fabric for every patch in the second layer. You may use three or four different fabrics for the second layer or all the patches may be made from the same fabric.

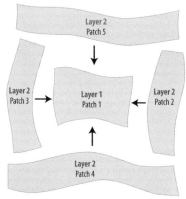

Sample of patch placement for a four-sided block. Layer 3 is added in a similar manner.

Planning for Patch 2

The seam allowance on the top edge of Patch 2 will be turned under and it will cover the raw edge of one side of the center patch (Patch 1). You may arrange Patch 2 on any one of the four sides of the center patch; it doesn't matter on which side of the center patch you begin to lay down the second layer patches.

The size of the patches should be at least 2½"–3" in width. They should be long enough to cover the length of one raw-edged side of Patch 1 plus have additional 2"-3" extensions of fabric on each end of the patches. The extra fabric, referred to as "extension tails" in these instructions, may either cover or lie beneath the ends of adjoining patches. If center Patch 1 is 4" x 6", then you would need to cut Patch 2 to be at least 3" wide by 8" long (to cover the 4" side) or 3" wide by 10" long (to cover the 6" side). If the center patch varies in width or length, adjust the measurements accordingly. You do not need to measure accurately any of the patches in a block, simply guesstimate the approximate width and length.

You are free to determine the overall shape of Patch 2 at your whim. As you cut a patch out of fabric, you may cut the bottom edge in a straight or gently curved line, or any other way you wish. It doesn't matter since the bottom of the patch will not show— it will be covered up by the turned seam allowance of a successive patch. However, pay special attention to the top edge of the patch. You may cut the top edge of the patch in a straight line or choose to sculpt the top edge of the patch with scissors, cutting the fabric in a random, curvy line. Once turned

under, the creased seam allowance on the top edge of Patch 2 is sewn down to the center patch; it is a seam line in the block. The creased seam line should have a pleasing, unique or unusual line or curve that complements the shape of the center patch.

Not only should the seams bordering the center patch be unique, so should all of the seam lines in the block. Interesting seam lines make for interesting blocks. Since there are no templates or patterns to follow as you cut out patches, allow your imagination to guide you. Let the edges and shapes of the fabrics you are using inspire you as you cut out the patches for the block. If you need inspiration for finding unusually shaped patches, here are several suggestions:

- You may use discarded or rejected patches that are left over after constructing a previous quilt.

- Consider a previously cut section of fabric used for other patches or quilts. Look anew at all the raw edges already present in the fabric. Are there areas with unusual edges or that have a pleasing line that can be lightly trimmed or sculpted to fit in the block?

- Cut out a patch at random in a free-form shape from a new piece of fabric (or scrap).

- Trace a specific shape on a piece of freezer paper to create a tem-

plate. Press the paper template to the right side of the fabric, cut it out and construct the patch as you did in Chapter 3, turning under the appropriate seam allowance.

Constructing Patch 2

1 Choose a medium value fabric or scrap for Patch 2. Cut out Patch 2 from the fabric with a pleasing top edge line and shape.

2 The long, top edge of Patch 2 will be turned under to form a seam allowance. If the patch has valley (concave) curves along the top edge, clip the seam allowance for ease in turning the seam under. The deeper you cut the fabric, the sharper the curve will be. If the seam line has mountain (convex) curves, especially a sharp curve, you may need to trim the excess seam allowance curve for a

smoother line. Starting at one end of the patch turn the seam allowance over and press with an iron a little at a time until the seam line is complete. Do not turn under any other edges of the patch.

3 Position Patch 2, right side up, so the crease of the turned seam allowance covers a raw edge on one side of Patch 1. You may arrange Patch 2 so it overlaps the center patch as little or as much as you wish, as long as the raw edges on that side of the patch are covered.

Position Patch 2 to cover the raw edge on one side of Patch 1.

Note: In the basic technique the edge of a freezer paper template is a guideline for clipping curves. You are able to make well-spaced even clips in the seam allowances. When working improvisationally, you do not have the benefit of a paper template edge to guide you and it is very easy to make the clips uneven. To get the curve to turn under in a smooth, even line, make a conscientious effort to clip the seam allowance at even intervals and at a consistent depth.

If you are not satisfied with the way Patch 2 fits on the center block, try moving it around to any of the other three sides of the block. Many times if a patch has a sweeping curved line or a deep concave curve you can maneuver it to cover the raw edges on two sides of Patch 1. Play around with the patch until you are happy with the way it looks and fits in the design. Have fun with this technique! Once you find a good place for Patch 2, pin it securely to center Patch 1 and the stabilizer with straight pins.

Remaining patches in the second layer

4 Choose a fabric for Patch 3. Following steps 1- 3, cut out Patch 3 and turn under the seam allowance on one side. Position Patch 3 so the crease of the turned under seam allowance covers the raw edge on the second side of Patch 1.

The extension tail of Patch 3 may either overlap or tuck under the extension tail of Patch 2.

The extension tail of Patch 3 may either overlap all or most of the extension tail of Patch 2 or you may tuck it underneath the extension tail of Patch 2. Pin Patch 3 in place on stabilizer.

Give yourself freedom to play with the patches. Don't hesitate to change their positions or switch them around on the center patch. If you do not like the way the extension tail of one patch overlaps the tail of a previously laid patch, then reverse the position of their tails. Tuck the overlapping tail of a current patch beneath the tail of a previous patch. You can intertwine the extension tails of one patch with another patch in any way you want to expose more of a favorite fabric or motif in the print. Experiment to your heart's content. Ultimately you must decide which arrangement pleases you the most and looks the best visually.

5 If you are using four patches in the second layer, cut out Patches 4 and 5 in turn and construct them using the same steps as above. Position Patch 4 on the third side of Patch 1, covering the raw edge of Patch 1 and overlapping the tail(s) of the second layer patch(es) already arranged on the stabilizer. Position Patch 5 on the fourth side of Patch 1, covering the remaining raw

edges of Patch 1 and the extension tails of other second layer patches. If you are using only three patches for the second layer (forming a triangular shape), position Patch 4 so that it covers the remaining raw edges of Patch 1 and overlaps the extension tails from the other two second layer patches.

Sewing down the patches

Once the second layer of patches is pinned in place you may sew them directly to the first patch and the stabilizer foundation. Use a machine blind hemstitch and matching or blending threads to sew down the patches. You may begin stitching the seam in one of two ways: Lock in the stitch at the start of the seam where it intersects another patch by sewing forward a stitch, reversing a stitch, and then sewing forward. Or, you may start sewing the seam from beneath the overlapping patch. For this option, remove a straight pin, if necessary, from the patch that overlaps the seam being sewn down. Gently lift and fold back the creased edge of the overlapping patch and begin sewing the seam. Once the seam is finished, reposition the overlapping patch to its exact spot and replace the straight pin to secure it. End the stitching for the seam in the same manner, either by locking the stitch or ending the seam under an overlapping patch.

60

As with my basic technique, the patches are sewn in the same order that you construct them. For example, Patch 2 is sewn to Patch 1, then Patch 3 is stitched to Patch 1 and over the extension tail of Patch 2. That order may change if you switched or reversed the extension tails of some patches with others while constructing the block. When deciding where to start the stitching, the most important thing to remember is that the patch that lies beneath all of the others must be sewn down first. Then the next patch closest to the bottom is stitched second. Follow that sequence until all the patches are sewn. The last patch to be stitched is the one lying on top of the others. This order applies to stitching down any layer in the block. The patches that are laid down first and on the bottom of a layer must be locked in place first. This sequence assures a smooth start and a flat block since the fabric in successive patches may stretch a bit as you sew.

6 Sew down all the patches in the second layer, beginning with the bottommost patch. As you stitch, make necessary readjustments to the patches, being sure all raw edges stay covered. Press with an iron to smooth the block. One by one, lift up the raw, unstitched edge of a patch and fold it back, exposing the unnecessary seam allowances and extension tails beneath it. Carefully trim away the excess fabric beneath the patch, but do not cut away the stabilizer.

Explorations

Intertwining the patches and layers in a block is visually exciting. You may do this by leaving a portion of the overlapping extension tail on either side of a patch unstitched as you sew its seam. Then, as you construct the next layer of patches, you can slip the extension tail from a new patch, which will have a contrasting value, beneath the tail of the earlier patch. Once the latest layer of patches is arranged and complete, you will finish stitching down the remaining seams of the previous layer first before proceeding to stitch the last layer of patches.

Leave some of the extension tails from Layer 2 unstitched. You can intertwine patches from the second layer into the third layer.

Lift back the patch and trim the excess fabric from the block. Do not cut the stabilizer.

It's easy to nip the surface fabric while trimming these seams; use your fingers as a barrier between the scissors and surface fabric. When trimming away two or more fabrics in a seam allowance it is preferable to stagger the layers of fabric.

If you cut the layers evenly it creates a ridge that will show on the front of your block after it is pressed. Press well with an iron on right side of block before continuing.

The third layer

At this point you may stop adding layers if you want a smaller sized block or you may continue adding a third layer of patches. For the third layer choose a dark value fabric to contrast with the medium value of fabric patches in the second layer.

The third layer is constructed in the same manner as the second layer. For this layer you may choose to use four to six (or more) fabrics, depending on the size of the block, the patches and how many patches it will take to completely encircle the raw edges of the second layer. The number of patches you use for this layer is at your discretion.

For the third layer, cut, press, turn under seam allowances and pin the patches so they overlap the raw edges of the second layer patches. In this last layer of the block make the patches at least 4"-5" wide. After stitching the patches in place, fold back the raw edge to expose the excess seam allowance fabric and extension tails. Trim away the unnecessary seam allowance fabric beneath the patches, but do NOT trim any width from the patch itself. You may need the extra width of a

patch to join it to another patch when you arrange the blocks on the quilt top. At this point you may trim away the excess stabilizer if this is your final layer on the block.

Explorations

You may choose not to add a third layer of patches to every block. An alternative is to make half of the blocks in the quilt with two layers of patches and half with three layers. Make the patches in the third layer at least four inches wide. Then, when the blocks are put together in a final arrangement, the remaining raw edge of a third layer patch on one block can be turned under to form a seam allowance. The turned under edge can be positioned to overlap another block containing only two layers of patches. That one patch will serve as a third layer to both blocks.

Making linings for light-valued improvisational patches

During the course of constructing value-contrasting layers of patches in a block, a layer of light-valued patches may overlap the previous layer of dark-valued patches. The underlying seam allowance of the dark patches may cause unwelcome shadowing through the light-valued patches.

To line a light-colored improvisational patch, you must create a freezer paper template for the lining. The first step is to cut out and construct the improvisational light-colored fabric patch as usual, turning under the appropriate seam allowance. Next, cut a piece or strip of freezer paper that is somewhat larger than the fabric patch and lay the freezer paper, dull side up, on a soft surface such as an ironing board or a flat surface covered with a soft towel. Lay the fabric patch on top of the freezer paper, right side up, so there is at least ½" of paper extending beyond the crease of the turned under seam allowance. Using a dressmaker's serrated tracing wheel, trace as accurately and closely as possible along the entire edge of the turned under seam so the notches in the wheel of the tool make indentations in the freezer paper template. If a patch has two sides with turned under seam allowances, then trace both sides.

Cut the template from the freezer paper, cutting exactly on the notched lines.

Use a serrated tracing wheel to mark the freezer paper template.

This notched line is the matching seam line for the light-colored patch. Cut the unmarked, remaining sides of the paper template so they are equal or slightly larger than the dimensions of the fabric patch. There is no need for an exact match along the other sides of the patch...only the notched edge.

Use premium white muslin or other similar fabric to make the lining. Position and press the freezer paper template on the lining fabric. Cut out the lining patch exactly on the notched line along the top edge using the paper template as a guideline. Cut the remaining sides of the patch as usual.

Remove the freezer paper from the lining patch and finish constructing and tacking the lining in the same manner as directed on page 45. The notched edge of the lining should fit snugly and smoothly against the crease of the improvisational light-colored patch.

Cut out the lining template on the notched seam line.

Making circular and oval-shaped blocks

In most linear improvisational block shapes, such as triangles and squares, the top edge of a patch or the patch shape itself is formed generally in a straight line or strip. This is true even if you cut a curvy line along the top edge of the patch. When constructing a circular or oval block, both the top edge and overall shape of a patch are cut into an arc or semi-circle. Working with arch-shaped patches will help you attain the rounded look you want for the completed block.

1 To construct a circular block, cut out Patch 1 in a circle about 4" in diameter and place it on a piece of stabilizer 14" by 14" or other appropriate size. Do not turn under any seam allowances on Patch 1.

When cutting all successive patches, cut the top edges in an semicircle or arc. Make the curve about the same depth in all of the patches within a layer.

Clip the valley seam allowance on the top edge of each patch to an even depth and turn under. Only the top edge of a patch is clipped.

2 Overlap a raw edge of Patch 1 with the turned edge of Patch 2. Continue adding patches to the second layer until all raw edges of Patch 1 are covered. There are usually three or four patches in the second layer. Continue as above to construct the third layer of patches. The number of patches in the third layer will vary depending on the size and shape of the individual patches within the layer.

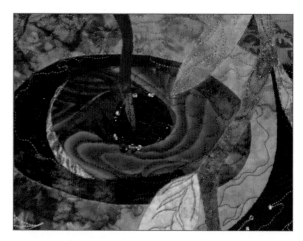

Oval block pattern from **The Promise of Spring**.

To make an oval-shaped block, proceed as above but cut Patch 1 in an oval or egg shape and place it on an appropriately sized piece of stabilizer. For the next and all successive patches, cut the top edge of the patch into a deeper or more acute arc.

While the general shape of a patch in a circular block is rounded and semi-circular, the patch shape for an oval block should be a crescent. Clip the valley seam allowance on the patch. Make the deepest cuts in the center of the arc and gradually decrease the depth and intervals of the clips to the tapered ends of Patch 2. Decreasing the depth and intervals of clips on the patch as the ends taper ensures the patch will retain its oval shape. Turn under the seam allowance of the patch. Overlap Patch 1 with the turned seam of Patch 2.

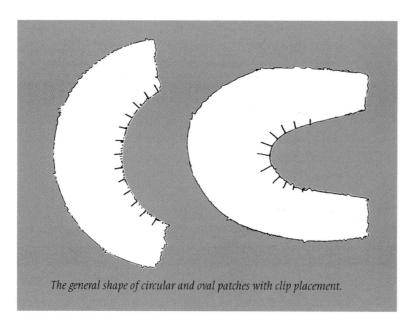

The general shape of circular and oval patches with clip placement.

Field Poppies

Turn under both sides of the corner angle on a quadrant.

Explorations

To make your circular blocks more interesting visually, make a few patches in Layer 2 shaped in quadrants.

Turn under the seam allowances on the angular edges of the patch and place on the center patch. Deliberately mismatch the points and seams on all layers.

Deliberately adding and mismatching points to a circular block breaks the monotony and adds a spark of curiosity.

Field Poppies, detail.

Continue by constructing Patch 3. Alternate the placement of the oval patches on either side of the center patch, making sure the tapered ends are long enough to overlap each other. Complete the second layer by positioning Patch 3 opposite to Patch 2, being sure it covers the remaining raw edges of Patch 1. The second layer is usually comprised of two, sometimes three patches. The crescent-shaped patches in the third layer are larger in size and their tapered ends longer in length. The number of patches in the third layer is usually two, sometimes three, if needed.

Cutting freeform oval patches with tapered ends can be tricky, especially when constructing the outer layers. For the most accuracy, consider making a rough sketch of an oval block on freezer paper and use the templates as a guideline for cutting the patches until you are more confident with this procedure.

Other helpful hints with this technique:

• There is an old cliché, "Variety is the spice of life." Variety within a composition also makes for more interesting art. Do not try to duplicate a previously made block, but vary the sizes and shapes of the blocks and the size of the fabric patches in them. Improvisational blocks do not need to be precise or symmetrical. Let the quilt take on a life of its own. Inspiration comes by working with scraps and freely cutting edges on fabric.

• Sometimes fabrics will have a motif or a pattern that must be placed in an upright direction (such as a flag or a cowboy on a horse) and you won't have a lot of flexibility when it's time to arrange the blocks into a quilt top. In these cases a design wall is helpful as you plan and construct the patches for each block. Once

you finish a block, begin to assemble it into a preliminary arrangement on the design wall. This will help you to determine where to place the colors and patches as you create the remaining blocks and it will maintain a sense of color balance in the overall quilt.

• When pressing fabric for a patch, iron it well with steam or mist before turning the seam allowance. Press it again after stitching each layer to help eliminate stretchiness in the fabrics and ensure a smooth block.

• In addition to trimming away excess fabric after stitching the layers, there is another option for eliminating surplus seam allowance fabric during the construction process. Position the new patch on top of the previous layer. Once you are satisfied with its placement in the block but before you pin it down, run your fingernail or the serrated tracing wheel along the seam line. This creates an indentation line in the fabric below. Fold back the new patch, trim away the excess fabric on the bottom layer, leaving a ½" or so seam allowance from the indented line. Reposition the new patch on the indented seam line and pin in place. Try both methods of trimming away the excess fabric in your block and use whichever one you find easier.

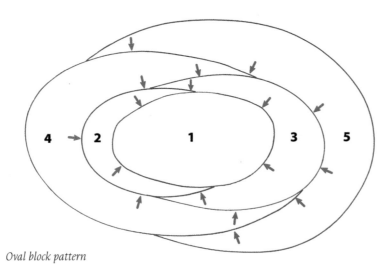

Oval block pattern

Preliminary layout of the blocks

Ultimately the blocks will be attached permanently to a stabilizer foundation. But first you must have a general idea for the preliminary layout of the blocks and a final shape for the quilt. At this point in the construction process, you have the opportunity to move the blocks around at will to decide on the most pleasing arrangement. You will use your own judgment, intuition and personal taste to settle on an arrangement for blocks in the quilt top. After you decide on the best positions for the blocks, simply attach them together with straight pins. Then the blocks are moved carefully to a stabilizer foundation where they will be pinned securely and permanently sewn down.

Begin the preliminary layout of the four blocks, playing with their arrangement. Keep in mind and apply the basic rules of color and design as you work with the blocks. The final arrangement should have flow or rhythm, have harmony or pleasing symmetry, have contrast and visual balance in color and proportion.

Always work with a design wall whenever possible. If you do not have a design wall, hang a piece of felt on the wall to serve as a design area, use drafting tape to attach the blocks to a wall or spread the blocks out on the floor. Arranging the blocks and viewing

them from a distance will help you better analyze the contrasts, intensity and balance of colors, the shapes created by the blocks and the overall size of the quilt.

There are two strategies when planning the layout of your quilt. You can make and attach each block to another as you go or you can make several or all the blocks before attempting to arrange them together in a pleasing design. I've made improvisational quilts both ways with good results. I personally enjoy making most or all of the blocks beforehand and then designing the quilt.

Most of the time the finished blocks can be turned around or upside down, shifted or interchanged with other blocks to settle on a pleasing and balanced arrangement for your quilt top. It is much like working a jigsaw puzzle. The first step in determining the layout of the blocks is to spread them out on a design wall or the floor to analyze them for color balance. The colors should be distributed evenly throughout the quilt top in a pleasing arrangement. For instance, if two blocks have strong red patches in their outermost layer, don't position them so the red patches lie next to each other. Turn one block around so its red patch will be on the opposite side and away from the other red patch, or move the whole block to the opposite side of the design. Try to position the blocks to balance all the colors in this manner as best as you can.

If it is necessary to add a color to a specific location to achieve balance, then create a new patch in the color you need. Form the new patch as a tapered wedge or other interesting shape and insert it somewhere in that area to correct the balance. The patches, wedges and strips you add can have straight edges, angular edges or you can make the edges curvy. The shape of a wedge, strip or block can be changed at will and adjustments made as needed to cover raw edges.

Depending on how you arrange the blocks, the overall shape of the quilt can vary, forming a square, oval, diamond, circle, or triangle. Also, blocks can be arranged in a straight line, asymmetrically staggered or placed in an "S" shape. As a general rule, the largest or visually heaviest block should be on the bottom of the quilt top. In planning the heart of the design or center block in the arrangement, choose between your favorite block, the strongest or brightest colored block or a distinctly important (focus) block. Small blocks can be either sandwiched between the bigger blocks or be placed around the outer edges of the quilt top.

The blocks shouldn't be too close or on top of each other, and should have enough "quiet" space between them to be distinct and defined. In other words, a plain fabric should lie between two busy or printed patches. If your outermost layer is a themed or

busy printed fabric, simply add another layer of dark, quiet fabric between the blocks to separate the two printed patches and define the shapes of the blocks. This will also serve to make the two prints stand out even more. Choose a non-busy fabric for the new patch that will not compete visually with printed patches in the outer layers of the blocks. Cut the new fabric in the shape of a strip, triangular patch or wedge, turn under a seam allowance and pin the strip between the blocks. Do not sew the new patch onto a block at this time. Don't worry about the gaps between the blocks as you arrange them. The gaps can be filled in with additional fabric patches as needed once the blocks are transferred to the stabilizer.

Attaching the blocks to one another

The blocks can be attached to each other in two ways.

1 The raw edges of a patch in the final layer of a block can be turned under to form a seam allowance. The folded seam is positioned to overlap the raw edges of a final layer patch in an adjoining block and pinned in place. There is no rule of sequence or order for turning under the raw edges of one block when arranging it with another block. For example, if you are putting two blocks side by side and aren't satisfied with the way a turned under edge of Block 1 looks when it overlaps Block 2, you could reverse the order and instead turn under the seam allowance of Block 2 so it overlaps the raw edge of Block 1.

2 Another intermediate fabric is introduced. The new fabric patch can be shaped as a triangle, strip or wedge and it lies in the middle between the two blocks to be joined. Both long edges of the new patch are turned under, forming seam allowances that will overlap the raw edges of the blocks on either side of it. Pin the new fabric in place.

Turn under the seam allowance of a third layer patch on one block to cover the raw edges of an adjoining block.

Cover up open spaces between blocks by adding another patch of fabric, such as a wedge.

68

The final arrangement

Once you are happy with the preliminary arrangement of blocks, you can transfer them to a large piece of stabilizer foundation. Cut a piece of mid-weight stabilizer somewhat larger than the approximate size of the preliminary arrangement. To enlarge stabilizer foundations, please refer to page 50. Press the stabilizer smooth.

It is very important that the stabilizer is flat. If possible, pin the stabilizer to the design wall so it is stretched out and taut. Pin around the edges of the stabilizer to hold it in place. If a design wall is not available, tape the stabilizer to a flat surface.

At this point, your preliminary arrangement of blocks is held together loosely with straight pins. Carefully move the arrangement to the stabilizer and lay it on top, right side up. Pin the top edges of the arrangement to the stabilizer to hold it in place temporarily. Starting at the bottom of the arrangement, remove the pins from a block and press the block well and very flat to eliminate any potential stretch. Reposition the block to its place on the stabilizer and securely pin the block to the stabilizer. Be sure the block lies flat and as smooth as possible on the stabilizer. Neatness does count during this process to avoid stretch during the quilting process.

Unpin the next adjoining block or fabric strip and repeat the process, pressing it flat and repositioning it to its place on the stabilizer, overlapping the raw edges of the preceding block. Pin the strip or block securely to the stabilizer and the preceding block. Add new patches or readjust existing ones whenever necessary and turn under seams in whatever way you need to hide raw edges. Be sure every patch lies flat. If you run into problems trying to turn under both sides of a wedge with a sharp point, either blunt the tip of the point to a straight edge (simply turn under the point) if possible or refer to "Splicing seams" (see below). Continue pressing and attaching each block, strip and wedge to the stabilizer in this manner until the entire arrangement is pressed and secured to the stabilizer foundation.

Splicing seams

When working with my topstitch method, the natural flow of construction is to turn under seam allowances in the same direction. However, when introducing a new patch, a situation may arise where the seam allowances on both sides of an acute narrow point, such as a wedge, must be turned under. Turning under narrow points can be difficult. This dilemma can be solved by using an easy splicing technique. Splicing seam allowances will get you out of many a troublesome situation.

Begin by creating a paper template for the new patch. Insert a piece of freezer paper so that it lies at least one inch under the edges of the patch to be spliced, and one inch over the raw edges of any other abutting patches. This will allow for including seam allowances on all sides of the new patch. Make a hash mark (single straight line) at any point above the spot where the new patch must overlap the raw edge of the existing patch. Use a pencil to mark both the freezer paper template and also the adjoining patch. This mark indicates the point where the seam allowances will intersect.

Insert a piece of freezer paper so that it lies at least one inch under the edges of the patch to be spliced, and one inch over the raw edges of any other abutting patches.

Using a serrated tracing wheel, trace in the ditch along the seam already turned under on the patch to be spliced. Immediately after you cross the hash mark, begin adding a proposed seam allowance to the freezer paper tracing. The indentations from the tracing wheel will appear on the freezer paper, clearly indicating a stitching line. You must make certain that wherever the proposed seam lines are traced, the raw edges of all existing patches are adequately covered.

The seam allowance is handled differently on either side of the hash mark. The seam allowance will be clipped at the hash mark on the new patch and the seam allowance on one side of the clip will be turned under, but left raw on the other side. The raw-edged portion of the new patch will slip under the already turned under seam allowance of the existing patch. On the other side of the hash mark, the seam allowance of the new patch will be turned under and will cover the raw edge of the existing patch.

Make notations on the freezer paper template indicating which edge is turned under and which edge is left raw. Mark "raw" on the edge to be inserted under the turned seam allowance of the existing patch. Mark with arrows the edge where the seam allowance needs to be turned under. Also, mark with arrows any seam allowance that must be turned under on adjoining patches.

Mark the template on either side of the hash mark.

Cut the freezer paper template for the new patch on the notched line and press it to the right side of the fabric. Cut out the fabric patch, leaving seam allowances on all sides. Make a clip in the seam allowance, aligned directly with the hash mark. Before clipping the hash mark, fuse a small piece of interfacing on the wrong side of the fabric in the marked area to eliminate fraying at the cut. Turn under the seam allowance indicated by the arrows.

Turn under the seam allowance marked by arrows.

70

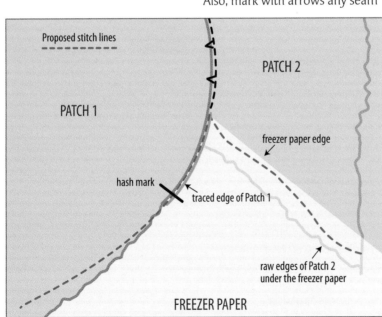

Trace the boundaries of the new patch to include seam allowances.

Proposed stitch lines
- - - - - - - - -

PATCH 2

PATCH 1

hash mark

traced edge of Patch 1

freezer paper edge

raw edges of Patch 2 under the freezer paper

FREEZER PAPER

Intersect the two patches at the cut, positioning them so the turned edge of one patch tucks under and covers the raw edge of the other. Adjust the patches so they fit snugly at the hash mark clip. Pin in place. Use a machine blind hemstitch to join the patches, sewing from the center outward in each direction or using a mirror image of the blind hemstitch. When the patches are stitched, the splice will be undetectable.

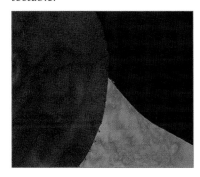

Once sewn with blending thread, the splice is undetectable. This illustration with contrasting thread shows how the seam is stitched.

Most times only the new patch needs to be clipped at the hash mark—the turned seam of the existing patch slips nicely into the cut and interlocks. However there may be times you will need to clip the hash marks on the seam allowances of both patches to interlock them and obtain a good fit. If you must clip the hash marks on both patches, prepare each patch exactly the opposite of the other patch so the raw edge of one patch corresponds with the turned under allowance of the other on either side of the hash mark.

Sewing the quilt top

After the blocks and patches are flat and securely attached to the stabilizer foundation, you may sew them down using a machine blind hemstitch and matching or blending thread. Begin stitching in the same order that you attached the blocks and wedge, if added, to the stabilizer. As you stitch always be sure that the blocks and patches are lying flat on the stabilizer and that there is no give or stretch between them. Stop after sewing down several patches and press them flat before you continue stitching the next set of patches. Reposition or readjust blocks or patches when necessary to eliminate any excess stretch that appears during the stitching process. Once the quilt top is completely stitched, press it well. If you see any patch that is not lying flat and smooth on the stabilizer, it is best to remove the stitches, smooth, press, readjust and restitch the patch. Otherwise, you may have problems with the area during the quilting process.

Is it finished yet?

When you work with improvisational techniques, quilts take on a life of their own. How it will hang when it is finished is a concern. There are some things you need to think about before you consider the quilt top finished and start the quilting process. Hang the quilt top (before sandwiching) on your design wall with a straight pin and check out different ways to hang it. Does it hang well? Does the quilt top weight seem centered and balanced? Does the quilt hang in a pleasing shape? Can the perimeter shape of the top accommodate a hanging sleeve or is it too uneven? For abstract designs, check all different positions and ways to hang the work. Sometimes it only takes a small shift to one side or the other to find the best position. Other times it may come as a surprise that the quilt is at its best turned upside down! At this step you might find it necessary to add more patches to balance the quilt before quilting.

71

Playing with the final shape

After the top is quilted the next step is to determine a final shape for the quilt. You certainly may finish the quilt in a standard shape such as a square or triangle, but this is a wonderful opportunity to fashion a quilt that is totally unique and eye-catching. The perimeter of the quilt can mimic the shapes of the improvisational blocks. Place the quilt top on a design wall and consider its present shape. Its current outline is unplanned and random. Look for any unusual angles, curved lines or other interesting shapes. Think about exaggerating and/or incorporating these unexpected, serendipitous shapes into the final shape of the quilt.

Make a temporary frame from drafting tape on the edges of the quilt or use a fabric marking pencil and flexible curve as you consider possibilities for the perimeter of the quilt. The lines of the outer perimeter may be angular or box-shaped, curvy, or a combination of both styles—curves mixed with angular lines. Finish the quilt using my fast finish envelope binding as described on page 156. Attach a hanging sleeve (page 164) and label, if desired.

Augie's Quilt, *in the collection of Augustine and Richard Ellis. Let the improvisational blocks inspire the final shape of the quilt.*

72

Improvisational sheer overlay

Another fun way to make an improvisational quilt is to lay down overlapping raw-edged patches of cotton and sheer fabrics at random on a foundation. The layers are secured in place on the quilt top by overlaying them with a large piece of sheer fabric, which is then quilted using free-motion stitching. This is an especially wonderful technique for depicting ice, water and sky. To demonstrate this technique, we'll use my quilt, *Winter's Hostage.*

Choosing fabrics

Decide on "base" fabrics for the "ice". The best choices are very light and medium-dark batik fabrics. Color selections might include blue, violet, gray, some pale yellow or aqua or even a touch of rust. You need to exaggerate the value contrasts for the base fabrics. Keep in mind that the sheer overlay will lighten and soften the appearance of the batik fabrics, and you want to achieve visual contrast despite the softened transformation.

Also, include some interesting sheer fabric for the ice. Translucent organza and polyester sheer fabrics are good to work with. Select colors for the sheer fabrics similar to the "base" choices and don't be afraid to experiment with dark-colored ones as well. Reflective hologram lamé or sheer fabric, when available, is fun to use. This fabric reflects color beautifully and stands out prominently in the quilt, even when covered by the overlay sheer fabric. This is one fabric I always enjoy including in my work!

73

Winter's Hostage *has two single layers of sheer fabric overlaying the patches in the quilt top to simulate ice. The sweetgum leaf is trapped between the two sheers.*

Layering the base fabrics

Begin with a 22" x 20" piece of stabilizer for the foundation. Press it smooth and lay it on a flat surface. Select the cotton base fabrics at random. Hold the first fabric in front of you. Place your hand about two inches down from the top edge and on the side of the first fabric. Scrunch a length of the fabric into your palm. The length should be around 8" to 10". Grasp the wad of fabric tightly in your fist. Use sharp scissors to chop off the excess fabric on either side of your fist.

Overlap the jagged strips, making sure no stabilizer is visible beneath them.

What a fun way to cut out patches...simply grasp a wad of fabric in your fist and chop off both ends!

The more jagged the cuts, the better. Unfold the fabric. You should have a long strip of fabric with jagged long edges on the top and bottom. Since both side ends of the strip are probably still straight-edged, cut them jagged as well. Press the fabric and place it right side up on top of the stabilizer.

Repeat this procedure with another fabric in a contrasting value and/or color. Try to vary the width of the strip. Once the second strip is cut, press and place it on the stabilizer so it slightly overlaps the previous strip. Don't worry about turning under raw edges with this method. Your only concerns are that the stabilizer doesn't show and the widths of the fabrics that do show are varied and contrasting. Continue making strips from the fabrics in varying widths and lengths. As you lay them down,

stagger the jagged strips so they do not appear to lie all in a row. Cut some of the sheers in the same manner and intersperse them among the other base fabric strips.

Once the strips are arranged to your satisfaction, you may tack down some of the larger cotton strips either to each other or to the foundation stabilizer with small bits of fusible webbing. Press the quilt top, using a large piece of parchment paper as a press cloth.

74

Adding the leaf

The sweetgum leaf with stem in *Winter's Hostage* was traced onto a piece of freezer paper using a real leaf picked from a tree in my backyard. The leaf measures 7" tall by 9" wide. The accompanying stem is 4" long. You may use a copier machine to reproduce a real leaf or draw your own. I cut out the leaf template from the freezer paper and pressed it to the right side of a rusty colored batik. The leaf was cut from the fabric and placed on the quilt top in the lower left corner of the quilt top. I scattered some colorful metallic threads on the quilt top and staggered a narrow strip of sheer fabric across the leaf before finally topping the quilt top with the sheer overlay.

Add decorative threads if desired and layer a piece of sheer fabric over the base strips to secure them. Use two layers of sheer fabric for a more subdued look if you wish.

Explorations

Because *Winter's Hostage* is a small quilt, each layer of the sheer fabric overlaying the patches on the quilt top is one solid piece. For a different visual effect and especially with larger quilts, you may use several pieces of sheer fabric instead of only one to overlay the patches. If you choose to use more than one piece of sheer as an overlaying fabric, you might consider using a heat tool to sear and curl the raw edges. (Refer to page 119 for this procedure) This will give dimension and texture to the design. Also the searing keeps the fabric from fraying.

In addition, because there are breaks between the sheer overlay patches, a design component, such as a leaf, can breach the overlay, with part of the leaf lying on the surface of the quilt top. The leaf would be divided, part of it lying beneath one patch of sheer overlay and the remainder exposed and lying on top of the adjoining patch of sheer overlay. The result is a wonderful visual effect for your quilt.

If a leaf patch lies totally beneath the sheer overlay, having raw edges on the patch will have little impact over time. However, if a portion of the leaf will be exposed on the top of the quilt, you must make it stronger and give it more stability. If you plan to use this technique in your quilt you have two options for constructing the leaf patch.

The first possibility is to fuse two pieces of leaf fabric, wrong sides together, with fusible webbing to form a single patch of fabric. Press the freezer paper leaf template to the fabric and cut out the leaf along the edge of the template. Because the two leaf fabrics are fused together, some fraying on the raw edge may happen eventually, but it will be minimal and not impact the appearance of the leaf. The second option would be to face the leaf patch as described in Chapter 5.

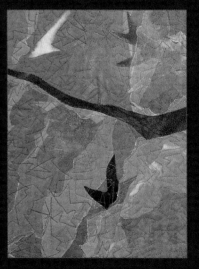

Life Beyond, *detail. A portion of this leaf breaches the layers of sheer fabrics and is exposed on the quilt's surface.*

Adding the overlay sheer

The next step is to decide on a sheer to overlay the quilt top. Experiment with the sheers you have to see which one gives the most pleasing appearance to the quilt top. You may even use two layers of sheer fabric as overlay if you wish. Usually you want to use something transparent. Milky or translucent sheers tend to obscure the base fabrics too much and your wonderful effects are lost.

Once you select a sheer fabric, you may either press it smooth or press in a few wrinkles using a parchment paper press cloth. Cut a piece of fabric larger than your quilt top. Lay the sheer fabric over the quilt top, either smoothing it flat or keeping the wrinkles intact if you pressed them in the fabric. Secure the sheer overlay well to the foundation using numerous straight pins.

Quilt the quilt top as desired. This is the perfect time to experiment with metallic threads. As with selecting colors for fabrics, you may choose metallic threads in any pastel color such as lavender, yellow, blue, aqua, silver, or use a variegated thread if you like. The stitch selection I used for my free-motion stitching on *Winter's Hostage* is the zigzag stitch rather than the usual straight stitch. The jagged zigzag stitch seems to fit better with the ice and mood of the quilt.

The jagged borders

The borders on this quilt were added after the quilting process so they are not quilted. I chose a batik fabric that contained not only most of the colors in the ice, but also quite a bit of the leaf color as well. Including the leaf color in the border helped to tie in and balance the leaf with the rest of the quilt. Also, the rusty color in the surrounding border fabric definitely enhances and draws attention to the leaf, which is the focus of the quilt.

The cotton batik border fabric has a sheer overlay as well. The borders were made in strips, partially faced and added to the quilt top one at a time. Both side borders were constructed and laid down first, then the top and bottom borders made and laid down, overlapping the corners of the two side borders.

To make the border, begin by choosing the cotton fabric for the border and the sheer fabric for the overlay. You will also need a blending fabric for the facing. Layer the sheer on top of the cotton fabric, with right sides up on both fabrics. Press the two fabrics together. Lower the iron temperature if necessary to accommodate the sheer fabric. Next, layer the facing fabric on top of the sheer, right side down. The right sides of the sheer fabric and the facing will be together. After pressing the three fabrics as one, pin the layers together securely.

Decide on a shape for the border. You may either design a border strip with a zigzag pattern on one long edge on freezer paper or you may cut and sew improvisationally. If you decide to work improvisationally, cut the fabrics as one into a strip approximately 19" long by 6" wide or to whatever dimensions you need for your quilt top. Be generous! Face the improvisational strip by sewing the fabrics with a narrow seam allowance along the top edge of the patch, incorporating jagged angles, waves or a straight line as you stitch. Keep the stitches smooth and even.

If you choose to use a drawn freezer paper template for the border strip, simply press the template to the wrong side of the facing fabric and sew the fabric layer together along the top edge of the strip using the edges of the freezer paper template as a guideline.

Once the top edge of the strip is sewn either improvisationally or using a template, trim excess allowance and clip valley curves. Fold the facing to the back, exposing the sheer fabric. Gently straighten the seam line, poking out any curves or angles and press.

Position the border strip on the side of the quilt top with the turned seam allowance overlapping the quilted surface of the quilt top. Blind hemstitch the border strip in place with matching thread. As you stitch the border, make sure the bite of the blind hemstitch is catching both border fabrics and not just the sheer fabric. Continue constructing the remaining border strips in this fashion and sewing them to the quilt top.

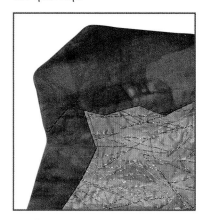

Once the border strips with sheer overlay are attached to the quilt top, you may slip snippets and narrow strips of additional sheer fabrics or strands of thread between the sheer fabric overlay and the cotton fabric. Including snippets and threads will add depth to the borders as long as there is some contrast in color and value. Smooth the two fabrics and press the borders well. Either pin or use bits of fusible webbing to tack the outermost edges of the layered border fabrics. You want to keep the slippery sheer overlay fabric in place, flat and joined to the other border fabric until you can determine the outer shape of the quilt and finish it. If you do use fusible web to tack the fabrics, tack only in two-inch intervals and no deeper than ¼".

Finishing the quilt

Determine the final shape of the quilt. Consider making the outer edges of the quilt either curved or angular to complement or mimic the inside edges of the border seam lines. Mark the perimeter of the quilt with a fabric pencil. Use a basting stitch to sew around the entire quilt top on the marked line. Take care as you sew that the sheer fabric lies flat and is not puckered. Lay the backing fabric, right side down, on top of the right side of the quilt top. Press smooth. Pin the layers together and finish with the envelope backing, page 156.

I hope this chapter on improvisational quiltmaking will become one of the highlights of your adventure. Break free from the block of traditional thought and become creative! Among the benefits of making unusual quilts and those with irregular or free form shapes is their uniqueness. Simply, these quilts are different from all the rest and stand out among the others. It is an expression and comment on your style. Take time to explore each path and enjoy every day of your journey.

77

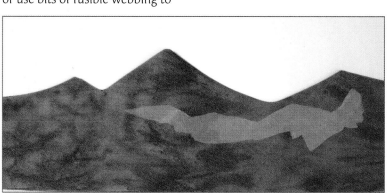

Use my facing technique to join and secure the sheer and border fabrics. Insert tidbits of threads and sheer fabrics to enhance the border.

5 Exploring dimension

Fabric manipulation allows you to use your hands and skills to alter and enhance a piece of fabric that will be used to make a wall quilt with dimension and texture. Making a quilt with manipulations is truly an exercise in free-form design—fun and always a surprise. It is similar to creating a mystery quilt because you have no idea how it will look until it is finished. You find yourself making changes in your work at every step and will see your quilt take on a life of its own. Remember the only rule is that there are no rules!

He Loves Me, He Loves Me Not, *detail.*
Above, **On Pins and Needles**.

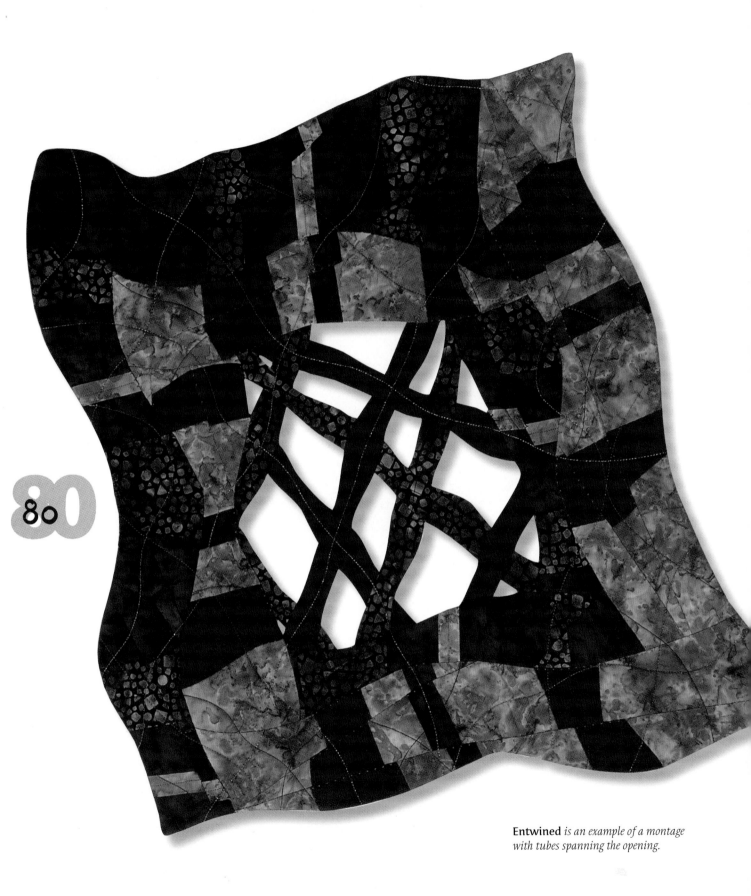

Entwined *is an example of a montage
with tubes spanning the opening.*

Fabric manipulations

The options I am presenting to you are only the tip of the iceberg. Let your imagination soar! Explore. Play. Experiment with your own ideas. The possibilities with this type of improvisation are unlimited. The manipulations in this chapter include strips, multi-fabric strips, pleats, tubes, wrinkles and facings. Fabric manipulation means to change or distort the shape and appearance of a piece of fabric in order to add dimension and texture to your quilt. Once the strips, pleats and tubes are made, they can be utilized in your quilt many different ways.

1 Manipulations may be arranged directly on top of a sandwiched and quilted quilt top, referred to as a **quilted base**. The surface of the quilted base may be either whole cloth or pieced. Once attached, the manipulations are quilted in a different direction or motif or even left unquilted for more dimension.

2 Arrange and stitch the manipulations at random on a large piece of quality quilting fabric used as a base or **fabric foundation**. The fabric is used in place of stabilizer. Once the fabric foundation is complete with manipulations, it becomes a **montage**, an assembled composite piece of artwork containing many overlapping or overlaying components. The montage is then cut into pieces or strips and used to make your quilt top.

3 **Whole cloth**, a large, single piece of fabric, may be pleated, wrinkled or folded and used as the background in a quilt top or as a focal area in a large expanse (ocean, sky, etc.). Or it may be used as a fabric foundation for the manipulations.

4 Using Pellon™ stabilizer as a foundation, the manipulations can be applied directly on the stabilizer. All raw edges of a manipulation are overlapped.

Dreamcatcher, *detail.*

Choosing fabric for the manipulations

Before you begin working on the manipulations in this chapter, give some consideration to the types of fabrics you choose. I tend to use mostly cotton fabrics in my quilts but you should think about including metallic or lamé and various sheers. You may use any type of fabric for these manipulations; however, I suggest you begin by using a stable cotton for your fabric foundation and choosing thinner or lightweight fabrics for the manipulations whenever possible. Be wary of using velvet, denim or other thick fabrics. Thick layers may be difficult to work with.

Once you learn how to make the manipulations in this chapter, you can work with satin, sheers, silks, and other filmy fabrics in your montage or quilt top for unusual effects. Sheer fabrics do not necessarily need to be stabilized. If they are folded in half and inserted between pleats, for instance, there is no need to stabilize them unless you choose to. The seam allowances on both sides of a sheer strip can be simply turned under and stitched to the fabric foundation. The raw edges will most likely show through the sheer material and may even add visual interest to the quilt. You may also sear the raw edges of a sheer patch or strip for texture and to prevent raveling. Another option for a finished look is to overlay the sheer on top of a cotton fabric and treat the two fabrics as one as you turn under the seam allowance. The sheer will add a gossamer look to the cotton fabric beneath it and the seam allowance will be hidden. If you are using sheer, silk and metallic fabrics for tube manipulations, I strongly suggest applying fusible interfacing to the back of these temperamental fabrics because the stress of turning the tube inside out will pull the fabric at the seam and it may rip.

Before you begin constructing the manipulations, decide what type of foundation to use.

The quilted base

There are endless design possibilities for arranging strips, pleats and tubes and sewing them directly to the surface of a sandwiched and quilted quilt top. It is a fast, fun and easy way to express your creativity! When considering what type of surface to use for the quilted base, think of simple options. One suggestion is to use a single piece of fabric as a whole cloth background that enhances or complements the manipulations. This is the simplest and easiest choice.

Another option is to construct a pieced top for the quilted base. For example, you might piece vibrant sunset colors together in wavy strips for the quilted base. Make the manipulations that will lie on the surface either in black or from a dark color. When the manipulations are combined on the quilted base, the end product will be a design in silhouette. Whatever you decide, make certain your choice for the quilt base complements the fabric for the manipulations and isn't too busy or distracting. For best results I recommend that you keep the design for the manipulations simple, using a single type of manipulation.

82

83

Sunrise Silhouette
Here tubes were arranged and sewn to a quilted quilt top.

Dimensions for the quilted base should be slightly larger in length and width than the size of the finished quilt. Remember, you will experience some shrinkage during the quilting process and while adding the envelope backing. Once you decide whether to use a whole cloth fabric or to construct a quilt top for the quilted base, you will use that piece to make a quilt sandwich and then free-motion quilt the entire layer.

Make the quilted base by using a large sheet of Pellon™ stabilizer on the bottom (enlarging the stabilizer if needed, see page 50) thin batting or flannel in the middle and the whole cloth fabric (or constructed quilt top), right side up, as the top surface of the sandwich. Keep in mind if the batting is too thick it will be difficult to stitch through when you combine the quilted base with the manipulations. Secure the sandwich layers together with safety pins and quilt the sandwiched layer as desired.

Using a fabric foundation for manipulations

The fabric foundation is constructed using a whole cloth. A whole cloth becomes a fabric foundation when manipulations are added. It does not have a stabilizer foundation. The material used as the fabric foundation is a key element in the quilt. The completed manipulations are spaced at irregular intervals across the fabric foundation, and much of the foundation is visible. Therefore, the color you choose for the fabric foundation will be a significant color in the finished quilt. Any high-grade cotton fabric is suitable for the fabric foundation, as are silks, metallics, hand-dyes or commercial cloth.

Balance and contrast are important in choosing fabrics for this technique. If the fabric foundation is a plain or subdued material, make some manipulations from printed fabrics. Similarly, if you choose a foundation fabric with a prominent print, counterbalance the busyness with mostly plain manipulation fabrics. In this way, the fabrics will not compete with each other. Vary the light and dark values when constructing the manipulations for the montage fabric. Using even small amounts of lamé or metallic fabrics and high-contrast or complementary colors adds zest to your montage. As you choose the fabrics to include in the montage, use your design wall to pin up and "audition" the fabrics that show promise. Seeing the fabrics and colors together from a distance will help you with the selection process.

You may decide to use only one montage fabric for your quilt or you may construct several different montage fabrics, cutting strips or shapes from all of them and intermingling them. Because of the variables involved with different manipulations, it is difficult to recommend a specific size for the fabric foundation. As an approximate frame of reference, I usually begin with a fabric foundation at least 20" wide and 44" long (the crosswise width of a bolt of fabric). If you make an entire quilt from only one montage fabric, make the fabric foundation wide or large enough to accommodate the intended size of the quilt. Once you decide on a size for the fabric foundation, press it smooth with a hot steam iron on cotton setting.

Explorations

In place of using a smooth fabric foundation, you might consider wrinkling the fabric in the foundation before adding the manipulations. Mist the fabric lightly, press, and the wrinkles will hold.

Simple strips

Making simple strips is the easiest manipulation. Cut out a strip on the crosswise grain of the fabric. The crosswise grain runs perpendicular (at a 90° angle) to the selvage edge of the fabric. Strips cut on the crosswise grain have more stretch. The curvy seam allowances will turn under better and the strip will lie flatter on the fabric foundation.

Use a rotary cutter and mat to make a straight strip or simply cut the strip with scissors at random with varying waves or curves on its long edges. If the strip is intended for use on a fabric foundation, cut the length of a strip to match the length of the foundation.

Strips can be any width you wish, but when figuring the width for a strip, be sure to include at least an inch or so for the turned under seam allowances on both sides. The finished size

Strips can be either straight or curvy. Turn under the seam allowances on both long edges of a strip and place it on either the fabric foundation or quilted base.

of a strip can vary in width from as little as ½" to 4" (or larger). Clip any valley curves on the seam allowances. Turn under the seam allowances on both long edges and press with an iron.

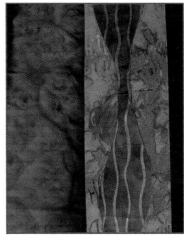

A second strip can overlap or be centered on the first strip.

Explorations: more thoughts about using strips

Add contrasting strips to strips pleated lengthwise.
Refer to page 106 for instructions.

- The surface of the strip does not have to be flat. You can iron wrinkles or pleats lengthwise in the strip if you want more texture or dimension. You may also add contrasting strips within the folds of the strip.

- Once a strip is stitched on both long edges to a fabric foundation or quilted base, a tube or second, narrower strip of contrasting fabric can be layered, straddled or centered on top of it.

- You can make a strip containing multiple fabrics.

Multi-fabric strip units

In this manipulation you will cut between three and ten strips from assorted fabrics and join them together lengthwise to produce a unit of cloth comprised of colorful strips. The unit is fabric only; there is no stabilizer foundation used for this manipulation. The unit is then cut crosswise or on a slant into secondary strips. Cut in this fashion, each crosscut strip will contain small portions of every fabric.

This technique differs from conventional methods for strip piecing. The traditional way to strip piece is to match the right sides of the fabric strips and sew a straight seam on the wrong side. All the strips have straight edges when the unit is completed.

With my technique, the strips are joined to one another by turning under a seam allowance, then overlapping the strip to the right side of a previous strip, and joining them by blind hemstitching on the top side. You can make the strips straight, or you can sculpt the strip by cutting the lengthwise edges into curved, wavy or angled lines. Sculpting the edges makes each strip unique and the curves and angles vary the width within the strip.

Choose up to ten different fabrics for the strips. Remember as you choose fabrics to maintain contrast in color, value (light/dark) and also in pattern (solid/pattern)—not only between fabrics

adjoining each other but also within the quilt top as a whole.

Strips are cut on the crosswise grain of the fabric. The width of a strip can be any size you choose, but be sure to vary widths among the strips. As you figure the width to cut a strip, take into account several factors. If you incorporate waves and curves in your strips, you will need to allow extra width to make up for space lost from overlapping seams and hiding raw edges. Don't forget to include width to each strip for the turned under seam allowances.

Although the strips may be different widths, they should be equal in length. The length of the strips depends on what you are making with the multi-strip unit. If you are making a quilt top consisting mostly of multi-color strips, then cut a 44" length for the strips. If you want just a few strips to add to your quilt top, then a 12" or 15" length will be sufficient for the strips.

Cut Strip 1, making it straight on both long edges. Do not turn under the seam allowances on this strip. Lay Strip 1 right side up on a flat surface. Cut fabric Strip 2. As you cut the second strip lengthwise, include curves, waves or angles only along one long edge to give the strip visual interest and character. Leave the other edge straight. Clip valley curves on the sculpted edge, turn under the seam allowance

and press the crease. Note that you turn under the seam allowance only on the sculpted edge. The other raw edge remains straight, flat and is not clipped.

Turn under the seam allowance on one long edge of Strip 2 and overlap the raw edge of Strip 1.

Align the two strips next to each other lengthwise, right side up, so the curvy, turned seam edge of the second strip slightly overlaps the raw edge of the first strip. When you are certain no raw edges are exposed, pin the two strips together.

Blind hemstitch with matching or blending thread to join the strips. Please note the fabric strips are stitched together without a stabilizer foundation. If you have a problem with the ends of the fabric strips getting caught in the throatplate when starting to sew a seam, insert a small piece of wax paper (or plain paper) under the fabric, extending about an inch above to ¾" underneath the fabric edges. The paper keeps the fabric stable until you can establish a seam line.

The needle-perforated paper will tear away easily when the seam is finished. Adjust the sewing machine tension so the bobbin thread does not show on the top. Use a walking foot for even feed.

After sewing the first two fabric strips together, press them so they lie smooth and flat and then flip to the wrong side. Trim away any excess fabric from the seam. Once trimmed, return the strips to the flat surface, right side up. Cut a third strip and turn under the seam allowance on one lengthwise edge. The turned seam allowance of the third strip may be positioned to overlap either the raw edge of Strip 2 or the remaining raw edge of the first strip.

A multi-strip unit can be sliced into individual strips.

The turned seam allowance of the third strip may be positioned to overlap either the raw edge of Strip 2 or the remaining raw edge of the first strip.

Pin, blind hemstitch, press the strips and trim the back as you did in the previous step. Continue this process with the remaining strips until you complete the multi-strip unit.

Once the multi-strip unit is complete, cut it crosswise or at a slant into secondary strips or use in patches.

As with other strips, you can cut the crosscut strips with straight, angular or curvy edges. The seam allowances are clipped when necessary and turned under according to how the strip is being used in the quilt top. The width that you cut a crosswise strip depends on how and where you use it. Before cutting a strip, take into account the amount of fabric needed for overlapping curves and angles, hiding raw edges and seam allowances.

Explorations: multi-strip units with pizazz

• Use metallic lamé fabric to make an individual strip. First, stabilize the fabric by using fusible interfacing on the back. Another option: wrinkle the lamé before you fuse it to the interfacing.

• A sheer fabric may be arranged to overlap a portion of a wide metallic strip. Cut the sheer fabric into a strip straight along one long edge and wavy on the other. Sear the length of the wavy raw edge of the strip with a heat tool. Once seared, the slightly curled edge is turned under at random as a seam allowance. Do NOT clip the allowance. The width of turned seam allowance will vary because of the waves you sculpted into the strip. Although the curled allowance is readily visible through the sheer fabric, it adds visual interest. Arrange the sheer fabric on the metallic strip so the turned under edge overlaps a portion of the metallic strip. To secure, stitch along the creased edge of the turned allowance using a straight stitch. Another successive strip will secure the remaining raw edges of the sheer and metallic strips.

• Cut one or more strands of colorful yarns and/or thick, decorative threads in a long length. Interweave or drape the thread or yarn across the front of the strips at random. Tuck a small portion of the strand into the strips' seams, pinning the strand in place as you go. When you sew down the strips, the thread will be secured as well.

Sear the long edge and turn it under to form a seam allowance. Overlap a portion of the sheer fabric.

Crisscross with colorful yarn and threads before stitching.

MANIPULATION 3:

Freeform pleats

The freeform pleat is an easy and versatile manipulation. If you had fun making pleated paper fans as a child you will enjoy this technique. The procedure begins with a simple fabric strip, cut on the crosswise length of fabric, long edges turned under. One narrow end of the strip is pinned to the top edge of the fabric foundation and then the strip is folded back and forth to form pleats.

Cut a simple strip of fabric with either gently curved or straight sides to whatever length and width you wish. Clip the valley curves on the long edges and turn under a generous seam allow-ance (⅝" to ¾") on both sides of the strip. Steam press to set the folds of the seam allowances.

Begin the pleating process by determining where you want the pleat manipulation to lay on the surface of the fabric foundation or quilted base. Start anywhere and work in any direction. Pin the raw-edged top of the strip, right side up, to the raw-edged top of the foundation or quilted base, right side up. Beginning about four inches from the top edge, grasp both edges of the fabric strip (width to width) and fold the fabric over onto itself to form a pleat.

Pin the fold to the fabric foundation or quilted base to hold it in place. Repeat the folding and pinning steps with the remainder of the strip to create a series of uneven, accordion-style pleats.

89

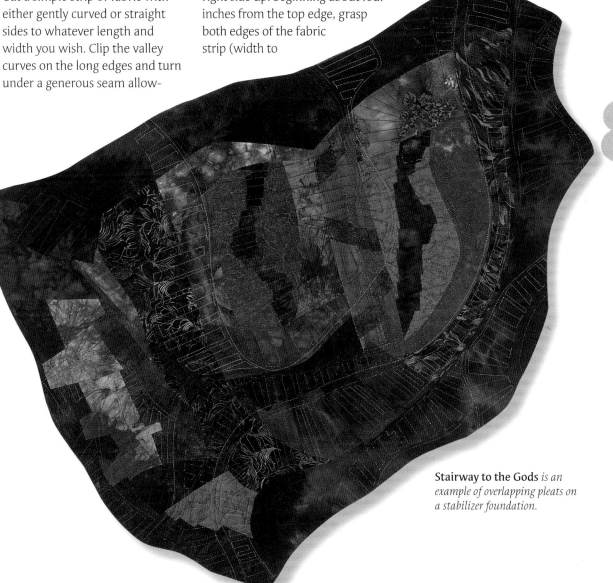

Stairway to the Gods *is an example of overlapping pleats on a stabilizer foundation.*

CHAPTER 5 | EXPLORING DIMENSION

If the folds are deep as you form each pleat, raw edges of the seam allowance can show from the back of the strip. If a raw edge is exposed, simply readjust the pleat shape to cover it. When the entire strip is pleated, press to set the folds.

The pleats do not have to line up straight, and the distance between the pleats can vary. Making each pleat a bit cockeyed so that it slants at different angles and varies both in thickness and distance is far more interesting visually than having all the pleats identical. If you want your line of pleats to be wildly slanted or cockeyed, the seam allowance will be visible. In these instances I make the pleats using a tube with two different fabrics (see page 93) eliminating the visible raw edges.

Creating a line of pleats uses a considerable amount of fabric, so you may run out of pleating fabric before you get to the bottom edge of your fabric foundation or quilted base. Leave the pleat length as is, or cut an additional strip of the same pleat fabric, turn under the seam allowances on both long sides and the top width of the strip and begin forming a new series of pleats. Hide the raw edges on the bottom of the previous pleat strip by overlapping it with the top of the new pleat strip.

Pin the pleat to the top edge of the foundation. Fold the strip over onto itself to form a pleat.

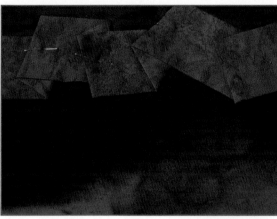

Make a line of pleats, securely pinning each fold.

To resume a line of pleats with a new strip of fabric, turn under the seam allowances on the top and long sides and position the new strip on the last pleat constructed.

90

Adding contrasting strips to pleats

If pleats are to be effective visually, there must be some contrast between them. If the pleat fabric does not have enough contrast, the creases in the pleats are not prominent and you won't be able to distinguish individual pleats. Individual pleats made from plain, light-colored fabrics are more visible than those made using a dark-colored or busier fabric. Also, how the pleats are attached to the fabric foundation or quilted base makes a difference. Pleats with only a light amount of stitching or stitching down the middle instead of on the folded crease have more dimension and are more visible than pleats that are heavily stitched or quilted. If you are not happy with the contrast you have with the pleats, you may add contrast. One of my favorite tricks is to slip in a thin, double folded length of contrasting fabric between the pleats.

Cut a strip of contrasting fabric the length of the pleat and between 1"-1½" in width or even wider depending on how much contrasting fabric you want to show. Fold the strip in half lengthwise, wrong sides together, and press. Position the strip so its raw bottom edges tuck inside the body of the pleat. Arrange the strip to show as little or as much contrasting fabric as you want, but try to vary amount that is exposed for visual interest. You can insert the contrasting strip in some or all of the pleats in the series.

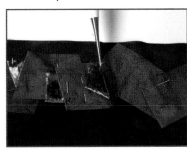

Contrasting strips help define and add interest to pleats.

Before stitching the contrasting strip, hide the raw-edged ends in one of three ways:

• Fold the raw end over the edge and beneath the pleat.

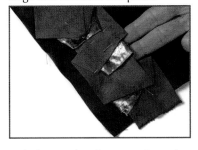

Hide the raw edge of a contrasting strip by tucking it beneath the pleat.

• Fold the raw end to the back of itself at a 45° angle. Trim the bottom raw edge on the turned portion of the strip so that it is the same as the rest of the strip.

Angle the end of a contrasting strip behind itself. Once the strip is tucked into the pleat, the raw edges are hidden.

• Taper either end of the contrasting strip by trimming the raw edges only on the bottom of the folded strip to form a sharp narrow point.

Hide the pointed end(s) in the body of the pleat or fold.

Angle the end of a contrasting strip and bury the tip in the body of the pleat.

Once the series of pleats is in place, pinned and pressed, sew them down on the fabric foundation or quilted base. There are several sewing options:

1 Stitch using two straight or wavy lines lengthwise down the long edges of the line of pleats. Stitch close enough to the edges of the pleats so any raw edges from turned seam allowances are not visible.

2 Using a straight stitch and stitching widthwise, sew a specific distance (e.g. ¼", ½", etc.) from the fold leaving the pleat's edge loose. The edges can then be manipulated or twisted the opposite direction during the quilting process for dimensional effects.

3 Sew down only the folded edge of each pleat with the machine blind hemstitch. This method works well if you are adding contrasting strips to your pleats. Be sure the raw edges of the

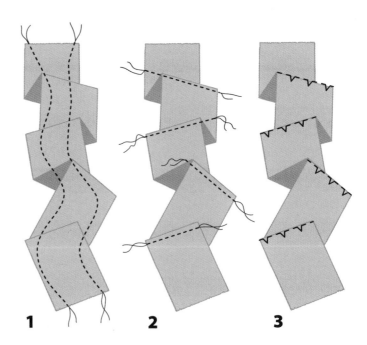

1   **2**   **3**

Pleats may be sewn down in several ways.

contrasting strips are tucked deep into the interior fold of the pleat and the line of stitching catches them. Stitching only on the pleat fold leaves the folded edge of the contrasting strip loose and dimensional, adding visual interest and texture.

If you are sewing the pleats onto a fabric foundation, once the sewing is complete flip the foundation over and trim the excess fabric from the seams on the back to avoid heavy fabric layers.

Explorations: Other ways to use pleats

•Fold wide strips into pleats or long wrinkles lengthwise.

•Cut one or more strands of colorful yarn or thick, decorative thread in a long length. Interweave the thread or yarn across the front of the pleats, tucking a small portion of the strand into the folds of the pleats. Pin the strand in place as you proceed. Stitch the folded edge of the pleats, securing the threads (left).

Another dimensional special effect you can use in your quilt is the tube. A basic tube is a strip of fabric folded lengthwise, right sides together, and stitched along the long raw edge. The tube is turned inside out to the right side of the fabric and pressed flat. There are no exposed raw edges on the sides of a finished tube so you can twist, turn or loop the tube on the fabric foundation and not worry about hiding seam allowances. You can make a tube from a single fabric or use two contrasting fabrics, one for the front side and one for the back.

You may construct tubes from fabrics other than cotton. I like to use metallic fabrics for texture and contrasting effects in my quilts. If you choose silk, lamé or other metallic fabrics, use a lightweight woven cotton fusible interfacing as a stabilizer. This will help prevent fraying and give the fabric body. When you make tubes and work with an additional layer such as the interfacing, take the thickness factor of the layered fabrics into account when deciding how wide to make the tube. A thick or interfaced fabric is more difficult to turn inside out when it is sewn in narrow widths less than ½".

There are several options for constructing tubes:

1 Simple straight-line tube
Begin with a strip of fabric. To determine the strip length, decide the length you want the tube to be and add 2". To determine an approximate width, decide the

width you want the tube to be, double that measurement and add an inch. The additional inch factors in the seam allowance. For instance, if you want to create a tube that is approximately 42" long and 2" wide, begin with a strip of fabric that is 44" long and 5" wide.

Cut a straight strip of fabric and press flat. Working on a flat surface or ironing board, lay the strip right side up. Fold the strip exactly in half lengthwise with right sides together. Press to set the crease. Sew a straight seam down the length of the raw edge using matching thread. The seam allowance should measure somewhere between ¼" and ⅜". When the tube is turned inside out, a tiny amount of width will be lost during the transition. Making the seam allowance just short of ½" will help make up the lost width.

Begin stitching by placing a small piece of wax paper underneath the end of the tube to stabilize the seam. After the seam is sewn, carefully remove the wax paper and trim away the excess seam allowance close to the stitches (about ⅛") and turn the tube inside out. Poke out and straighten the seam. Press to flatten the tube.

2 Tubes with two different fabrics
Begin by cutting two different strips of fabric that are the same length and width. When choosing fabrics for a two-sided tube, there should be a noticeable contrast

between the two fabrics. Then when you twist, loop or manipulate the tube there is more interest and visual distinction between the top and bottom. Place the strips on the ironing board, right sides together, and press smooth. Sew both long sides of the strip using blending thread. You can stitch the tube straight or wavy on both sides, or if you wish, curved on one side and straight on the other. You do not need to determine where to sew the seam lines before you start sewing. Sew the seams freely, stitching curvy lines and angles at will. However, do not sew the opposite seams too close to each other. If you do, the opening between them may be too narrow to allow you to turn the tube inside out easily. Trim the excess seam allowance close to the seam, clip valley curves and turn the tube inside out. Poke out and straighten the seams. Press to flatten the tube. For a variation, offset the seams when you press the tube, so that a narrow width of the bottom fabric is visible on the top of the tube.

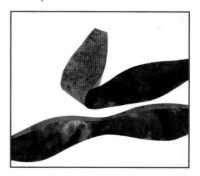

Tubes made with two strips of fabric may have wavy lines. Offset the seams for an unusual effect.

3 Zigzag tubes

An eye-catching manipulation is the zigzag tube. Follow the instructions for making tubes with two different fabrics (page 93). Cut straight strips from the two fabrics in the same width and length and place one strip on top of the other, right sides together, to form a two-layer strip.

Sew the tube's zigzag seams freely without marking them, or if you are not comfortable sewing improvisationally design a zigzag pattern for the tube before you stitch. To design a zigzag pattern, first draw it on the dull side of a narrow strip of freezer paper. Cut the design from the freezer paper on the drawn zigzag line. Press the paper strip to the top side of the two-layered strip along one lengthwise edge. Use the freezer paper edge as a guideline to stitch around the angles and complete the zigzag seam. To vary the zigzag pattern on the tube, design another line of zigzags for the opposite side of the two-layer strip or just simply turn the original freezer paper template around and press it to the other edge of the tube. The angular line pattern you just stitched will be in reverse.

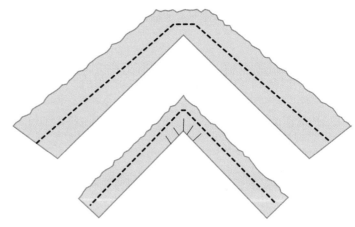

Top: For mountains, cut across the tip and down the slopes. Bottom: The valleys and deep "V" need deep clips to turn smoothly.

Whether you stitch a zigzag seam at random or design a paper pattern, vary not only the size and angles of the peaks in the zigzag design but also the width of the tube between the two zigzag seams. The peak of any angle shouldn't be too sharp. The seam allowance will cause the tip of the angular shape to be too thick to lie flat once the tube is turned inside out. It is wise to blunt the peak of an angle by stitching across the tip with one or two stitches to form a narrow, flat top across the top of the peak. Trim the seam allowance across the flat top of the angle and ¼" down each side of the peak so the tube turns inside out smoothly. Don't forget to clip the deep "V" angles in the seam allowance before turning the tube inside out. Poke out and straighten the seams in the tube. Press to flatten. Sew the zigzag tube on the fabric foundation or quilted base as desired.

A zigzag tube is an exciting addition to a quilt top.

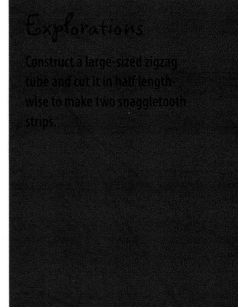

Explorations

Construct a large-sized zigzag tube and cut it in half lengthwise to make two snaggletooth strips.

4 Sheer fabric overlay tubes

Choose two or three fabrics for this manipulation. You will need two fabrics for the top side of the tube—a base fabric (such as cotton or lamé) and a sheer fabric (such as organza). Lay the base fabric down on a flat surface, right side up. Layer the sheer fabric on top of the base fabric. Be sure you like the overall effect. Depending on the sheer fabric, it will completely obscure, soften, brighten or darken the base fabric. Once you are satisfied with the base and sheer fabrics, choose a fabric for the bottom side of the tube. The bottom fabric can be either the same material as the base fabric on the top layer or a different cotton fabric.

Cut three strips—one strip of base fabric and one strip of sheer fabric for the top of the tube, and one strip of fabric for the bottom of the tube. Make all three strips the same dimensions. Press. Working on a flat surface or ironing board, sandwich the three fabrics in this order: the base fabric, right side up. The sheer fabric, right side up, is in the middle of the sandwich. The fabric for the backing of the tube is the top layer of the sandwich and is right side down. The sheer and backing fabrics will be right sides together.

Layering the fabrics for sheer overlay tubes. Offset the seams for an interesting effect.

Press to flatten and pin. Note that when working with a sheer fabric in a tube you may need to lower your iron temperature to avoid melting the fragile fabric. Stitch the tube as desired. Trim the seam allowance close to the seam, and clip valley curves. Turn the tube inside out, carefully separating the backing fabric from the base and sheer fabric layer. That way the sheer fabric remains on the front side of the tube and overlays the base fabric after the tube is turned inside out. Poke out and straighten the seams and press to flatten. Sew the tube to the fabric foundation or quilted base as desired.

5 Multi-fabric tube

Follow the directions on page 93 for "Tubes with two different fabrics" to construct a multi-fabric tube. For the top side of the tube cut a strip from a multi-fabric unit (page 86). Choose a plain fabric for the bottom side of the tube. The bottom fabric should have sufficient value contrast so that it stands apart from the busy top fabric.

Turning the tubes inside out

In all these tube manipulations, the tube is turned inside out after stitching. There are inexpensive notions on the market specifically for turning tubes, straps and narrow strips inside out and they are a useful item to have. I heartily recommend you purchase one—they are worth every penny and will save you hours of frustration!

If you decide to use this tool for turning fabric tubes inside out, please remember to adjust my instructions accordingly.

The hardest part of making tubes is pushing out the curves or zigzags and adjusting the seam(s) after the tube is turned inside out. Here is how I do it. Purchase a 3/16" wooden dowel at a hardware or craft store. Cut the dowel to about 18" long and taper one end with a pencil sharpener. Blunt and smooth the tip with an emery board so it won't be too sharp and tear through the fabric. Insert the tip of the dowel into the tube and gently drag it down the length of the stitched line. The dowel helps to poke out curves and angles and straighten the seam. Also, misting the fabric with water seems to help the process. Press the tube to flatten and set the seam(s). If a tube is folded and sewn with only one seam, the stitching line can run down one side of the tube or down the center of the back so it is not visible.

Once a tube is stitched and turned inside out, both long sides are finished. Depending on whether or not you stitched across the top end of the tube when you constructed it, either one or both of the ends are still raw-edged. Most times, having raw edges on the top and bottom of the tube will not present a problem. If the tube is joined to a patch, either the raw ends of the tube are turned under along with the patch's seam allowance or the tube's raw edges will be covered by a successive patch. If you want the tube to have a finished top edge, before you turn the tube inside out, stitch the top edge at the same time you sew the long side(s). Another option is to turn the raw edges on the top end to the inside of the tube. Smooth both turned edges so they lie evenly and stitch them together with a top stitch or hand whipstitch.

Arranging and stitching the tubes

Like other manipulations, tubes can be arranged anywhere on a fabric foundation or quilted base and they may be interwoven with the other manipulations. Be sure to vary the width sizes between tubes and other manipulations in the quilt to add visual interest. There are several ways to arrange the tube to the fabric foundation or quilted base:

• Pin the tube flat and straight on the fabric foundation or quilted base.

• Position and pin the tube so the top and bottom of the tube twists back and forth on the fabric foundation. This is very effective when tube contains two different fabrics.

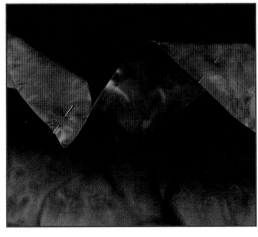

Tubes may be positioned to twist back and forth across the fabric background.

• Create small loops with the tube on the fabric foundation. Use a tube with either one or two different fabrics and space the loops at irregular intervals.

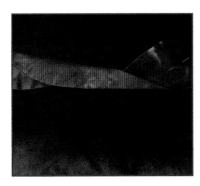

Tubes may loop across the fabric foundation.

• Use a tube with two fabrics for exaggerated or asymmetrical pleating.

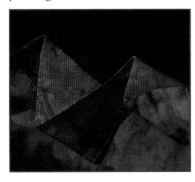

Accordion fold tubes for wild, cockeyed pleats on a fabric foundation or quilted base.

Attaching the tube to the fabric foundation or quilted base

• Sew the tube to the foundation or base with a single line of stitching down the center or on one side of the tube leaving the other long edge free.

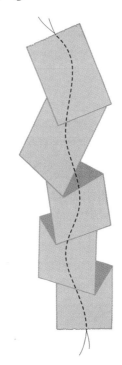

Pleated tubes may be stitched down the middle with a wavy line.

You may twist or manipulate the free edge for dimensional effect at a later time during the quilting process.

• Sew down the pleated tubes on the folded edge with the machine blind hemstitch.

• For twisted tubes or loops, blind hemstitch their edges where they lie on top of the foundation or quilted base, leaving the dimensional part of the tube unstitched.

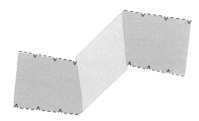

Blind hemstitch the edges of looping and twisting tubes where they lie on top of the foundation or quilted base.

4 Attach twisted tubes by tucking a corner or portion of the tube into the body of a pleat and secure the tube in place by stitching down the fold of the pleat.

Tuck a portion of a twisted tube beneath a pleat or other manipulation to secure it.

The pleat can be one from a line of pleat manipulations on the fabric foundation. Or, the pleat can come from pleating the fabric foundation itself.

Explorations

Entwined *(detail)* is an example of interweaving tubes in an opening in a quilt.

• In addition to sewing tubes to the quilt top or a fabric foundation, you can also use them to span openings in your quilt. (See above.)

• Experiment with shapes in the evening while watching TV. Cut multiple strips, crescents, arcs or other shapes out of inexpensive paper and arrange them at random into designs. When you discover a pleasing design, tape the paper strips together and save it as reference for a future quilt design.

• After arranging the manipulations on a quilted base but before stitching them down, insert a latticework of threads, yarn, etc. into the open space between the manipulations. Follow the directions on page 137. Insert the latticework so the raw ends lie under the manipulations and the threads are caught and secured when you stitch the manipulations in place .

Placing the manipulations on a quilted base

The potential for pattern designs using manipulations on a quilted base is endless. I enjoy sewing a variety of strips, tubes or similarly faced shapes on quilted bases. *Sunrise Silhouette* (page 83) and *He Loves Me, He Loves Me Not* (page 13) are examples of tubes and other shapes stitched to a quilted base. Tubes are particularly fun and versatile to work with. In addition to tubes fashioned in a straight or wavy line, they may be constructed in many other shapes such as crescents, elongated triangles, arches, S-curves, barrels, cones, semi-circles or any other shape you can imagine. You have total freedom to cut a tube into whatever length, width or shape you desire. This is the time to let your imagination run wild!

With the quilted base on your design wall, begin arranging the manipulations on the top surface. Use straight pins to hold the manipulations in place while you make design decisions. Arrange, overlap and interweave the manipulations at random on the quilted base in intersecting boxes of various sizes, triangles, circular or curvy lines or other design. Leave ample open space between the manipulations so the quilted layer underneath is visible between them. Remember to vary the sizes of the open spaces. As you arrange the manipulations, consider the balance of color and value within the design. When you are satisfied with the design and placement, securely pin the manipulations to the quilted base. For good results, be sure that the manipulations are lying perfectly flat and smooth.

Arrange the tubes as desired on the quilted base; attach them with a machine blind hemstitch.

Sewing the manipulations to a quilted base

Once the design is complete and pinned, sew the manipulations to the quilted base, using a blind-hem stitch and matching or blending thread. A walking foot is very helpful to negotiate all the fabric layers. You may need to adjust the bobbin tension because of the thick layers. Since the back of the quilted base is stabilizer, loosen the top thread tension slightly so it pulls just a bit to the back.

If the manipulation contains many colors and values of fabric, choose a blending neutral as the top thread. I tend to use light, medium or dark values of gray thread, which blend in well with most colors. The secret is to use a very thin weight thread for the least visibility. As you progress with the stitching, be sure the tubes lie smooth and fairly taut without ease.

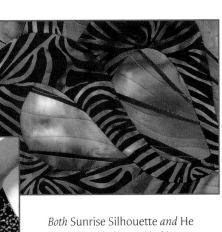

Both Sunrise Silhouette *and* He Loves Me, He Loves Me Not *are examples of tubes arranged on a quilted base.*

99

You have the option of quilting the manipulations now if you like or you can leave them unquilted. If left unquilted, the manipulations will appear to have more dimension. If you decide you want to quilt the manipulations, it is more interesting visually to use another color of quilting thread, quilt in a different direction or quilt with a contrasting motif pattern.

Determine the final shape and perimeter of the quilt and mark the binding line with a fabric pencil on the quilt top. Remember, your quilt may be any shape you wish, either with uneven or straight edges. Finish the quilt using the envelope finish technique as described on page 156 in Chapter 7.

Using montage fabric

If you constructed a fabric foundation, once all manipulations are sewn down, it becomes a created fabric or montage. Cut the montage crosswise or at a slant in straight or curvy strips for an unusual multi-fabric improvisational quilt. You may also use freezer paper templates to position and cut out patches from the montage fabric or just cut out strips at random.

When cutting the montage fabric into patches or strips, try to arrange the placement of the patch so that the most dimensional or bulky manipulations are centered or lie somewhere in the body of the patch rather than at the very edge of the patch. If the cut end of a manipulation dangles loose, secure it to the fabric foundation with a few stitches, or simply turn under both the seam allowance and the raw edge of the manipulation together as one.

If the montage fabric is cut into patches that will be layered in sequence on a stabilizer foundation, such as when using a pattern and my basic curves technique, turn under the appropriate seam allowances on the patches where indicated by small arrows. Press and pin the patches securely to the stabilizer. Make sure the montage patches lie perfectly flat on the stabilizer. Taking this precaution now will make a difference in the way the quilt hangs when it is finished.

If you are working with an improvisational method, turn under the seam allowance on a montage strip or patch wherever needed or where it overlaps another patch.

If you plan to put an opening in the quilt, then you must turn under any seam allowance on a strip or patch where it borders the perimeter of the opening. See Chapter 6, "Putting Openings In Your Quilt."

If the manipulations along the edge of a patch are too thick or unwieldy to turn under, the montage strip may also be faced before it is positioned in the quilt top. See page 107, "Facing shapes and patches."

Right: When the montage fabric is complete, cut it into strips or patches.

100

QUILTING BY IMPROVISATION

Wrinkling and folding a whole cloth fabric

The purpose of this technique is to add interesting texture to your quilt. There may be times you want a large, uncut expanse of a background fabric as a backdrop for a flower portrait such as *Oriental Poppy*. Your design may call for a large piece of focus fabric for the sky, ocean, water or other feature. In these instances you can manipulate folds, wrinkles and even pleats into one large piece of fabric to achieve movement, textural interest and unusual effects.

To achieve the best results with this technique, use a hand-dyed or commercial fabric that is primarily plain. The fabric should feature limited colors and widely spaced design elements, such as pattern lines created from the dyeing process. As a general rule, repetitive commercial prints such as calicos, batiks with a heavily printed design or other busy fabrics do not work well.

Remember that as you twist, warp and manipulate the fabric into wrinkles and folds the overall size of the fabric shrinks. The amount of fabric needed for the background depends on the size of the quilt. If you are wrinkling a specific area that is an element in the design, such as ocean or sky, take into account how much area the element will cover and plan accordingly. It is difficult to give a specific yardage for the wrinkling and folding manipulation because of the variables involved. Depend-

Oriental Poppy, *detail.*

ing on how heavily the fabric is wrinkled or folded, the size of the fabric could shrink between 15% to 50%. If your heart is set on using a particular fabric, don't underestimate the yardage you'll need before you begin. Be sure to allow plenty of fabric for the wrinkling process.

Before manipulating a whole piece of background fabric, consider splashes of color or other elements such as lines or a design created from the dyeing process that may be already contained within the fabric. Decide how you might position these components to balance the quilt and complement your focal point. This will make it easier to decide which area of the fabric should be on the top or at the bottom of the quilt. It may influence your ideas for the final shape and layout of the quilt.

You can manipulate the whole-cloth fabric in two ways:

Use the Surprise! element
Lightly dampen a large piece of fabric. Wait a few moments then spread it out loosely on the ironing board. Iron the entire cloth at whim, deliberately keeping the wrinkles and folds intact, pressing them with steam to set the creases. The fabric can be wrinkled or folded as narrow as ¼" or as deep as 1".

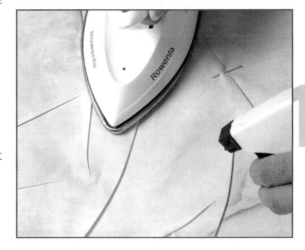

Mist with water and arrange the wrinkles in the fabric at random, pressing them. Then move the fabric onto stabilizer for support.

You can manipulate some of the folds to lie in different directions or into wavy curves. With this free and easy option, you never know what effect you may get and it may offer an unexpected creative inspiration that will affect the artistic direction you take. There are no mistakes. If you are not happy with what you come up, just moisten, rearrange and press the fabric again.

A more structured approach

is to dampen the piece of cloth and press it smooth. If the fabric is intended to be the background of the design, determine the location of the design's focal point. Start arranging the wrinkles and folds where you want them to be in relation to your design or focal point. For instance, if you wanted to create a flower quilt such as *Oriental Poppy*, decide first where you want to place the flower in the design. Next decide if you want the background folds to run beneath the flower or flow around the outside of the flower. If you want the wrinkles to flow around the outside of the flower, manipulate most of the folds to surround the area where the outer layer of flower petals will be placed. If the fabric is intended to be part of the focal point or other component, begin arranging the folds where you want them in that area. For instance, if you want to simulate waves in an ocean or water scene, you might create various sized wavy or rolling folds lengthwise in the main body of the fabric.

You can be flexible when working with folds or wrinkles. If the fabric you are manipulating falls a little short in a particular spot, extend its length by eliminating a fold or two or making the folds a bit narrower. For situations where the original fabric cannot be extended sufficiently, another option is to introduce a new fabric into the area. To do this, turn under a seam allowance along one raw edge of the new fabric. Use folds, wrinkles or pleats to integrate the two fabrics by overlapping the raw edges of the original fabric with the manipulations in the new fabric. Once added, the new fabric can be sewn to the original fabric with a blind hemstitch, a curvy straight stitch or free-motion quilting.

Because you don't want the added fabric to look contrived or as though you are trying to fix a mistake, don't try for an exact match to the original fabric. Instead choose a blending fabric with significant contrast from the original. Add balance by tying in the new fabric or a similar color in either another area of the quilt top or somewhere near the area where you added the new fabric.

Many times, less is more. Don't overdo the folds and wrinkles to get your point across or achieve the desired result. Unless you are going for a special effect that calls for heavily wrinkled fabric, keep the overall appearance of the fabric neat. Even though wrinkles and folds are pressed into its surface, the fabric should have a smooth, pleasing look to it. Put some pressure on the iron as you press the fabric to smooth out unnecessary wrinkles and to even out areas where the fabric is extensively distorted or not lying flat. A misting bottle is helpful to lightly dampen the area a bit before you press. For visual interest, always vary the lengths and widths of the folds.

Once the wrinkled fabric is manipulated to your liking, you must pick it up and move it to a stabilizer foundation. Since folds and wrinkles may shift during the move, use straight pins to hold the main folds in place while you make the transfer. If the wrinkled cloth is a whole cloth background, move it to a piece of Pellon™ stabilizer that is a few inches larger on all sides than the size and shape of the whole cloth. If the cloth is intended to be part of a pattern or design such as an expanse of sky or ocean that is already under construction, you do not need to cut a new piece of stabilizer for it. Simply move it to its position on the stabilizer foundation of the quilt top.

Once the fabric is moved to the top of the stabilizer or its place in the quilt top, secure the fabric, wrinkles and folds to the stabilizer with plenty of strategically placed straight pins, keeping everything in place and looking the way you created it. If the wrinkled cloth is part of a design element, integrate it into the quilt top by using the remaining patches in the pattern to overlap and hide the raw seam allowances around the cloth's perimeter. The seams from the surrounding patches and quilting will keep the whole cloth in place on the stabilizer.

104

105

The tree branch in **Hanging On for Dear Life** *is constructed using a wrinkling technique.*

If the wrinkled cloth is a background, you have two options to continue the quilt top:

• Attach and sew other elements to the whole cloth such as three-dimensional flowers, leaves, contrasting color strips or other manipulations. As an example, see *Oriental Poppy*, page 2. The whole cloth is not sewn directly down to the stabilizer. After the elements are added and the design is complete, the quilting secures it to the stabilizer. This option allows you work freely with the design, adding and eliminating elements, changing the wrinkles and folds in the background and letting the quilt top grow and develop. Quilting the background after the elements are attached is more difficult and you may not be able to quilt some areas of the background as heavily as you might like. However, you do have more freedom to design and change the appearance of the quilt top.

• A second option is to sandwich the wrinkled cloth and quilt it before adding design elements, using it as a quilted base and adding manipulations. *Sunrise Silhouette* (page 83) is an example. You may also add shapes and focal elements such as tree branches.

It is easier to quilt the whole cloth background before the elements are added. This is a better option if you want to quilt the background cloth a little heavier. However, do not quilt too much or you will lose the dimensional effect of the folds and wrinkles. While the quilting process may be easier, you do not have as much freedom to play with the design. You cannot adjust the folds or wrinkles, add contrasting color strips or make other changes once the background is quilted.

Adding contrasting color strips to wrinkled fabric

Wrinkling fabric is an exciting and fun way to put texture in your quilt. Besides adding texture, you may use the wrinkling manipulation to enhance the visual contrast even more by adding contrasting color strips to the folds. Because the inside areas of larger folds make excellent hiding places for raw edges, you can slip in small double-folded slivers or scraps of colorful or contrasting fabric. If visual contrast is missing within the wrinkled fabric itself, inserting contrasting color strips into the largest folds will help to separate and distinguish the folds ironed into the fabric.

I used thin violet strips in the background of *Oriental Poppy* (page 2) to achieve not only visual contrast within the background, but to get movement in the quilt as well. In an ocean or water scene, you might insert a lamé or sheer fabric among the curves to give the illusion of waves reflecting in sun or moonlight.

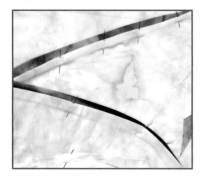

Contrast strips are added for visual interest.

Make a contrasting strip that will fit into the curvy folds and wrinkles of your fabric by cutting a narrow strip of fabric on the bias. Bias strips have more stretch and will be easier to conform to the shape of a curved fold. Depending on how much of the fabric strip you want to be visible, cut the strip one to two inches wide and as long as needed for

Add highlights and interest in an ocean scene with sheer contrasting strips.

the fold. Fold the strip in half lengthwise, wrong sides together and press. Most folds and wrinkles ironed into a whole cloth have a wider body in the center and ends that taper out to a sharp point. If needed, taper one or both ends of your contrasting strip to match and fit into the body of the fold. Taper the ends by trimming the raw edges only on the bottom of the folded strip to form a sharp narrow point. Hide the pointed end(s) in the body of the wrinkle or fold.

When inserting strips of fabric into the crevices, be sure to hide all of the raw edges on the bottom and the sides of the strips, tapering the ends of the strip to narrow

points that disappear in the fold. Stitch the wrinkle to secure the contrasting strip by using either a machine blind hemstitch or a straight stitch running down the length of the wrinkle's crease.

In general, the folds and wrinkles ironed into a piece of cloth do not need to be stitched down unless you have incorporated contrasting strips of fabric within them. The quilting process secures the folds. In fact you may not want to stitch them because in the course of creating the design you may wish to change the direction or placement of a wrinkle. I tend to rearrange the folds and to insert contrasting strips in the folds as the final steps in the creative process in order to balance the quilt colors and design.

Without a doubt you will end up with an oddly shaped piece of fabric after you distort it and iron in wrinkles and folds. At this point, if the fabric is intended to be a focal point or other element, the raw edges will be covered with other manipulations or patches. But if the wrinkled fabric is the entire background of the quilt top, as with my quilt *Oriental Poppy*, consider using the most pleasing, interesting or unusually shaped edges as part of the final shape of the quilt. A quilt doesn't have to be shaped like a box with straight sides. Oddly shaped quilts have become my trademark!

106

Facing shapes & patches

Once my topstitch technique was mastered, I continued to explore more creative possibilities and ways to make constructing a quilt with curves even easier. One of my proudest inspirations is to use facings, not only for patches on the quilt top, but also to bind and finish the quilt as well. Facings are a wonderfully easy approach for constructing smooth, finished patches for a quilt top when working with bulky layers of fabrics. Use facings to construct patches with hard-to-turn seam allowances, such as those with closely spaced wavy or curved edges, before adding the patches to the quilt top. Perhaps the most fun will be facing shapes, such as flowers and leaves, to give your quilt texture and dimension. However you use facings in your quilt, remember to explore your own creative possibilities!

Turning under the seam allowances smoothly might prove to be difficult for patches containing a lot of waves or sharp curves, such as an oak or poppy leaf. I've found that using lightweight cotton fabric as a facing solves this dilemma and gives an even, uniform look to the turned edge. Match the color of the facing fabric to the base color of the patch so the facing blends in well and isn't noticeable. Remember, you need not face all the patches...only the ones that are too awkward to turn under evenly. You can construct the facing for a patch so the entire patch is faced or only a portion of the patch is faced.

Partial facings

Because most patches are arranged on the quilt top in a sequential (one patch overlaps another) order, you may need to face only part of a patch. Face the top edge and part way down the sides of a patch, leaving the bottom edge open. Successive patches will cover the raw edge on the bottom of the patch.

If you are using a freezer paper template to make the patch, trace the original template in reverse on freezer paper. Reversing the template helps you to easily determine motif placement or directional flow on the patch fabric.

Cut out the new template and press it to the wrong side of the fabric patch. Place the patch face down on the right side of the facing fabric (right sides together, the freezer paper on top). Use

Sew along the sides and top of the patch using the freezer paper edge as a guideline.

the edges of the freezer paper template as a guideline to sew a straight seam along the top edge and down the sides of the patch.

Trim away excess seam allowance and clip valley curves. If desired, trim away some of the excess facing along the bottom edge. Turn the facing over to the back, straighten the seamline and press to flatten. Reposition and press the original freezer paper template to the patch. Return the patch to its place in the pattern and pin.

If a shaped patch was cut improvisationally, place the patch right side down on the facing fabric (right sides together) and sew both fabrics together with a narrow seam allowance along the top edge and sides, leaving the bottom edge open. Trim excess seam allowance and clip valley curves. Turn the facing inside out, straighten the seam line and press.

For improvisationally faced patches, sew along the top and sides of the patch, leaving a ¼" to ⅜" seam allowance.

Facing an entire patch

A situation may arise that leaves no choice but to face the entire patch. For instance, on *Oriental Poppy*, page 102 the full leaf, curvy on both sides, is fully faced.

If you are using a freezer paper template when cutting out the patch, trace that template in reverse on another piece of freezer paper to create a new template. Cut out the template and press it to the wrong side of the cut out patch. Place the patch right side down on right side of facing fabric (right sides together, the freezer paper facing you). Using the freezer paper template edge as a guide, sew a seam around the entire perimeter of the patch. Trim away excess seam allowance and clip valley curves. Make a lengthwise slit in the center of the facing. Take care not to nick the patch's top surface. Remove freezer paper.

Turn patch inside out, straighten seams with a plastic corner or blunt instrument and press well. Reposition the patch to its place on the quilt top. When a patch is in place on the quilt top or fabric foundation the slit in the facing will be hidden.

Note: If the direction the patch faces is not crucial, you won't need to make a new template for the facing. It will not make a difference in the outcome of the patch. The freezer paper can be pressed to the wrong side of either the facing or fabric patch. Then proceed with the remaining steps.

If a shaped patch was cut improvisationally, place the patch right side down on the facing fabric (right sides together) and sew a narrow seam along the entire perimeter of the patch. Trim the seam allowance and clip curves. Make a lengthwise slit in the center of the facing. Turn the patch inside out as above. Straighten seams, press and reposition the patch to its place on the quilt top's foundation.

To face the entire patch, stitch around the whole patch. Turn the patch over and make a small slit in the facing fabric.

108

The Promise of Spring, *detail. These three-dimensional flowers were faced and then added to the quilt top. They are secured with free-motion stitching.*

Three-dimensional faced shapes

While faced patches are integrated and sewn into the quilt top, I use a similar facing technique to make freestanding, three-dimensional flowers, leaves and other individual shapes that are added to the surface of the quilt top just before the quilt top is finished. See *The Promise of Spring (above)*.

To make a dimensional shape such as a flower, begin by drawing a flower shape on the dull side of freezer paper. Make the shape random and whimsical as in a child's drawing. Do not struggle to draw a perfect flower. Draw the flower as a single unit, but vary sizes and shapes of the petals within the flower. Set the drawing aside. Please note that with this

procedure, the completed flower will be the mirror image of the original drawing. Most times, it doesn't make any difference in the design. If you want your flower to be shaped exactly as your drawing, flip the drawing over and trace it in reverse.

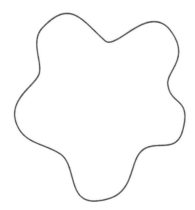

Draw a simple whimsical flower.

Choose a fabric for the flower and cut a square about two inches larger on all sides than the paper flower shape. Sandwich the flower fabric square right side up (top layer) with a square of flannel in lieu of batting (middle layer) and a square of stabilizer on the bottom. Cut out the flower shape from the freezer paper and press it to the right side of the flower fabric. Trace the shape of the flower to the fabric with a fabric-marking pencil. Remove the flower template and set aside. Quilt the three layers of the sandwich to mimic the veins of a flower. Quilt only around the outer edges of the petals, leaving a portion in the center of the flower unquilted.

The center portion will be stitched later when the flower is attached to the quilt. Once the sandwich is quilted, it is time to face the flower.

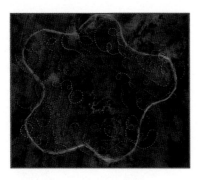

Free-motion quilt the flower, but leave the center area free of quilting.

Choose either the same fabric you used for the flower surface for the facing or pick a fabric in a blending or harmonizing color. Often I'll use a slightly darker hue of the flower color for the facing; the darker color on the back suggests a shaded flower. Cut a piece of facing fabric to match the size of the flower square and press well. Place the facing face down on top of the flower square so right sides are together and pin the edges. Press the flower paper template to the wrong side of the facing fabric, aligning its position as closely as possible to the tracing beneath the facing fabric.

Press the flower template to the top of the facing fabric.

Stitch around the entire perimeter of the flower with blending thread.

Once the outline is sewn, trim away all excess seam allowance close to the stitching and clip all valley curves or deep "V" cuts. Make an "X" cut in facing fabric in the center of the flower shape. Make this cutting as small as you can—just enough room to turn the flower inside out. Poke out and straighten the seams in the flower. Press. Place a snippet or small piece of fusible web between the stabilizer and inside of the facing to fuse the slit together.

Facing off-center shapes

An interesting technique to use on your quilt is to include faced shapes that are placed off center or that hang freely from the top edge, such as the leaves and flowers in my quilt *The Promise of Spring* (page 109).

Shapes can be positioned off-center so they hang freely from the surface of the quilt.

The procedure to make the shape is the same as above, but before layering the sandwich (surface fabric and flannel) and quilting it, decide which part of the shape will be sewn down to the quilt top. Leave this area unquilted when you free-motion stitch the rest of the shape. After stitching the facing fabric to the sandwich and trimming away excess allowance, make a slit in the facing directly under the unquilted area of the patch. By doing this, the cut will be hidden when the patch is sewn to the quilt. The slit should always lie under where you will attach the shape to the quilt top.

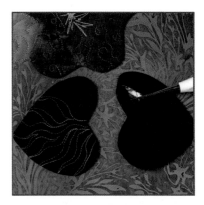

The slit should always lie under where you will attach the shape to the quilt top.

Plan accordingly and mark both the corresponding areas with pins or a fabric pencil.

Another way to quilt a faced shape

In some instances, rather than first quilting the layered sandwich and then facing the shape as described above, you may quilt the dimensional and faced shapes just before attaching them to the quilt top.

After the shape is faced and turned inside out, free-motion stitch around the outside of the shape first before attaching it to the quilt with more stitching. This procedure works well too, but there are limitations. You cannot quilt the shape quite as heavily this way, especially around outside edges. Also, it is not as easy to control and handle the smaller shapes under the machine needle during the quilting process. This method works well when you want only limited quilting on a shape.

Attaching dimensional shapes to the quilt top

The dimensional shapes may be arranged on the quilt top in three ways:

- on top of other patches already sewn on a pieced quilt top,

- on top of a quilted, *whole cloth* background that has a stabilizer foundation and will be finished with an envelope backing,

- hand sew the dimensional shape to a finished quilt.

With *The Promise of Spring,* adding the violets and other flower and leaf shapes to the grassy bank was the final phase of constructing the top before sandwiching the quilt with a backing fabric and free-motion quilting it.

Attach the flower to a background by positioning the flower as desired on the front of a quilt top. Secure the flower to the quilt by free-stitching the unquilted area of the flower. Use contrasting threads if you wish to simulate a flower center. The quilting usually covers enough area so that if you were to lift the edges of the flower, the underside is perfectly finished and you shouldn't see any sign of the cut you made in the facing fabric. Finish the flower center with beading if desired.

Secure the flower on the quilt top by free-motion stitching the center with contrasting thread. Beading adds a charming touch to the flower centers.

If you opt to include other three-dimensional faced shapes, such as leaves, to accompany the flower, position the leaf beneath one of the flower's petals. The portion of the leaf hidden beneath the petal must be the area with the slit in the facing. The slit is secured when the flower and leaf are stitched. Wherever the flower overlaps a leaf, use a machine blind hemstitch to stitch the flower to the leaf (and foundation). Use thread that matches or blends with the flower. You may secure any portion of a three-dimensional shape to the stabilizer by stitching along the shape's edge with a blind hemstitch, but keep in mind that the point of facing a shape is to achieve dimension. If you sew down most of the shape to the foundation you will defeat the purpose.

111

Some of the willow leaves in *The Promise of Spring* hang loosely from their tips. The narrow leaves were constructed like a tube with tapered ends rather than the faced shapes described above.

Create a dangling leaf by making a long, narrow sandwich. Use a piece of stabilizer or flannel as the bottom layer, fabric for the front of the leaf, right side up, as the middle layer and fabric for the back of the leaf, right side down, as the top layer. The size of the sandwich ranges from 6"-10" long, depending on the length of the leaf, and about 4" wide. The stabilizer gives body to the leaf. Use flannel instead of the stabilizer for a thicker leaf.

Draw a leaf template on freezer paper, tapering the bottom end of the leaf to a blunt point and narrowing the top portion of the leaf to about ¾" to allow room to turn leaf inside out.

112

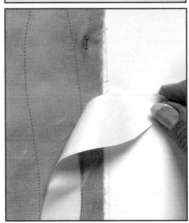

All the leaves in **The Promise of Spring** *(right), were cut improvisationally. This pattern is the general shape I used for the leaves.*

Press the paper leaf template to the back of the top layer (the leaf backing fabric). Stitch around the perimeter of the leaf, leaving the top of the leaf open. Trim the excess seam allowance, turn the leaf inside out through the open end using a tube turning tool. Free-motion stitch veins into the leaf. Attach the leaf to the quilt top, hiding the raw edges by covering them with another patch (the tree branch).

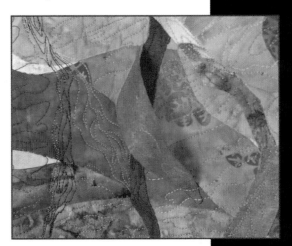

Secure the raw edge of the leaf with another patch, such as a tree branch.

Portrait of a poppy

Facing multiple patches for a dimensional flower

With *Oriental Poppy*, I wanted to portray a three-dimensional flower with multiple petals on a wrinkled, whole cloth background. Since I wanted the flower localized in a particular area with no raw edges showing, I needed to face each of the petals and arrange them using improvisational pleats and manipulations. Because this is an improvisational process, there is no pattern, but these instructions will help you create your own flower design.

Begin by choosing fabric for the flower. The back of the petals will definitely be seen when viewing the quilt. The flower should have visual excitement, texture and color contrast. Use different fabrics on both the front and the back of the petal to achieve value contrast; however, it is not necessary to use different fabrics in every petal throughout the flower. Choose a lighter color value for the front side of the petal. Use either a shade of the front of the petal or some other harmonizing color in a deep value for the facing or back. Exaggerate the color value contrast of the flower from the center to the outer petals so the viewer sees a distinguishable flower, not just a mass of color. It

Left: **Oriental Poppy,** *detail, is an example of a dimensional flower in a quilt. (Full quilt on page 2.)*

doesn't matter if you work from dark in center to light on the outer petals or vice versa. The choice is a matter of creative preference.

Next, choose a harmonious whole cloth fabric for the background. The whole cloth background fabric is wrinkled and pinned to a stabilizer foundation. As a guideline, I began with a piece of background fabric measuring 36" wide and 36" long for my quilt, *Oriental Poppy*. The background fabric was only lightly wrinkled and most of the folds in the fabric were not deep. After the wrinkling process was completed, the background fabric measured approximately 29" wide and 34" long. Most of the wrinkles and folds in my background fabric were made lengthwise (from top to bottom), so I lost more area in width (5") than in length (2"). Allow for a 15% to 50% shrinkage in overall size depending on the number of wrinkles and the depth and size of the folds you incorporate into your background fabric. The average loss will be about 30%. Wrinkling the background cloth is a manipulation process and is described in detail on page 103. Please refer to those pages for information regarding choice of whole cloth fabric, the procedure for wrinkling whole cloth, and how to move it to a stabilizer foundation. Also, refer to page 106, "Adding contrasting color strips to wrinkled fabric".

Begin your flower by cutting strips for the outer petals. Create each petal shape individually and at random, cutting the petal patch out as a strip but with a slight arc.

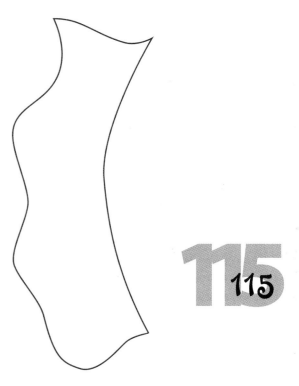

Cut the petals improvisationally. Make them curvy on the top and arched on the bottom.

Cut the top edge of each strip in a wavy line and vary the length of the petal strips. My poppy was constructed with a total of six petal strips, three for the outer layer of petals and three for the inner layer. The finished poppy is 12" in diameter. I cut the initial strips for the outer petals of my flower between 16" and 22" long and about 6" wide.

115

Facing the petal strip

Since each petal is three-dimensional it is necessary to face the top and sides of each petal (see "Partial facings", page 107). Choose the facing/backing fabric and put the flower petal fabric face down on the facing, right sides together. Smooth and press.

Construct the partial facing by stitching a curved line at random across the top edge and down both sides of the petal unit, leaving a narrow seam allowance of about ⅜". Where the line of stitching on the top edge meets the sides of the petals, you may either round the corners or extend and exaggerate a corner into a point to give your petal character.

If you exaggerate the corner, do not stitch to a sharp or narrow point; blunt the tip by taking two or three stitches across the tip. The blunted point turns inside out more easily and looks better when the petal is finished. Trim the seam allowance close to the seam line. If you make a point on your petal, trim the excess seam allowance across the tip and down either side of the tip before turning the petal unit inside out. Clip valley curves and turn the facing to the back. Poke out curves and points with a blunt tool and straighten the seams. Press.

Facing for hanging petals

If you want the sides of some petals to twist, spiral or hang away from the main body of the flower, continue stitching the facing down one side of the petal and include a couple of inches along the bottom edge of the petal. Make a straight clip in the seam allowance at the point where the stitching ends on the bottom of the petal; the seam will lie more smoothly once the patch is turned inside out.

By stitching the seam allowance a couple of inches on the bottom of the patch, the exposed bottom portion of the petal will have a finished appearance. If you wish, twist or position the finished side and bottom of the petal into a spiral and secure it to the background or extend the petal to hang freely beyond the other petals. The remaining raw edges on the bottom of the patch will be covered by another petal later.

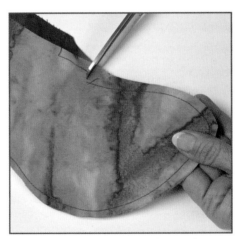

Left: Have fun sculpting the petals. Round some corners and exaggerate the points on others. Above: Stitching the bottom of the petal part way allows you to spiral the petal once it is turned inside out. Don't forget to clip the seam allowance for a smooth finish.

116

Positioning the outer petals on the background

The three finished, faced strips I used for the outer layer of poppy petals in *Oriental Poppy* ranged in size from 14" to 20" long and 4" to 4½" wide. Before making the flower you must decide its placement in the quilt. Next determine how far out the outer petals of the flower will reach on the background. That spot is where you will begin to lay down the outside edges of the outermost petal strips. Pin the side of the faced petal strip to the background, positioning it with the curvy side out and the raw edges of the strip pointing toward the flower center. Manipulate the strip into very gentle pleats at random, forming an arc. Pin the pleats to the background as they are formed. Remember to vary the pleat size. The pleat sizes should not be identical.

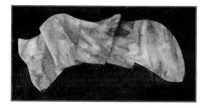

Begin arranging the outer layer of petals in a circle on the background fabric.

Finish the end of the strip by letting it lie flat or, if you faced some of the bottom edge, curl the side end to either the back or front, forming a whorl or spiral and giving the petal more dimension.

Twist the end of the petal into either a forward or backward spiral for more dimension.

Continue creating and pleating outer petals until the entire outside row of petals is complete and in place. At this point you have two options. Either stitch the outer petals down with free-motion quilting now, or continue finishing, arranging and pinning all the remaining petals in the flower and then do the stitching. It is a little more difficult to stitch the outer petals with the center petals

pinned to the background, but you have more leeway to arrange and tweak the flower's appearance to your liking if you wait to stitch the whole flower.

When free-stitching the petals to the quilt top, begin stitching the outer petals first and stitch each inside row of petals in turn until reaching the flower center. For individual petals, work from the raw edges at the bottom to the top of the petal. Stitch back and forth in long, wavy lines.

The petals take very little quilting to secure them to the background. If you quilt the petals too much, you'll counteract the very effect you are trying to achieve—dimension. Keep the quilting to a minimum with most of the stitching limited to the area just above the raw edges and in the lower center area of the petal. Only a few stitching lines should reach near the top edge of the petal. Be sure there are no raw edges showing on the facing.

It does not require much stitching to hold the petals in place. Too much stitching will lessen the dimension.

117

The inner layers of petals

As you cut the strips for the inner layer of petals, decrease both the length and width of the patches as you work toward the center of the flower. The flower becomes more compact in the center and you have less area to cover. I cut the initial three strips for the inner petals of *Oriental Poppy* approximately 13" to 15" long and 4½" wide. The finished, faced size of the petal strips ranges from 12" to 15" long and 2½" to 3" wide.

When forming the second row of petals, arrange them in an arc with the outer layer. Begin laying the second row just inside of the outer row of petals. The center area of the second row petals should be directly above the raw edges of the petals in the previous row. Placement is the same for subsequent petals until reaching the flower's center.

Position the inner layer of petals so that once they are stitched down, they will cover and secure the raw edges of the outer layer of petals.

If fabric thickness is a problem, trim away a small amount of facing (½" to ¾") from the bottom of a petal (the raw edge) to alleviate some of the bulkiness. Trim only the facing, not the petal fabric. Be sure not to cut off too much facing or you'll be unable to hide the raw area on the back of the patch when stitching down the petals.

I used six petal strips in my flower, but you may use as many as you like or need. Leave an empty area in the center of the flower, a circle about an inch in diameter for the fringe and flower center.

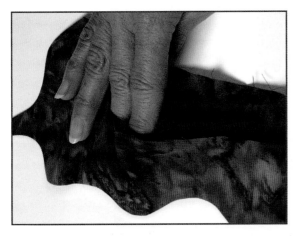

Trim off a small amount of facing fabric from the bottom of the patch if thick layers are a problem.

Once the second layer of petals is ready to be stitched, again start at the raw edges on the bottom and stitch mostly in the center, with only very few quilting lines reaching the top edge. The main function of the stitching is to cover and secure any raw edges on the petal row that are lying below the new petals being stitched. As you stitch a petal, check underneath it often. Bend the top of the petal forward to see whether any raw edges are visible. This will enable you to see where and how far up into the petal you must stitch to hide the raw edges in the petal row that lie underneath.

If you want heavily quilted flower petals and yet retain the dimensional aspect, free motion quilt the petals before you face them. To stabilize the petal fabric for stitching, layer it on top of a piece of stabilizer and quilt the area that will be the top edge of the petal. Keep the bottom area of the petal relatively free so you can attach the petal to the quilt top with additional stitching. Once the petal is quilted, face it and proceed with placement on the quilt top as described above.

118

The center fringe

I constructed the fringe around the flower center in the *Oriental Poppy* quilt by layering two circles of sheer organza fabrics—black and violet. I cut out a circle from each fabric, and then cut part way into the circle. I seared the sheer fabrics with a heat tool to shrivel the raw edges, prevent fraying and create a curly, ruffled look.

Cut one 4" circle from purple organza fabric or sheer and a 4½" circle from black organza. Make snips halfway into the circle on each fabric.

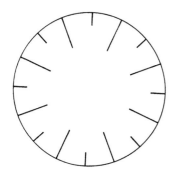

Cut out two circles of sheer fabric for the poppy fringe. Cut snips into the circles.

Working on a Teflon™ surface, sheet or ironing board cover, use a heat tool to singe the raw edges. Always use long needle-nosed tweezers to hold the fabric in place while working. The tweezers keep the fabric from shifting or blowing away and keep fingers out of the intense heat. If you've never used a hot air gun, please practice a few moments with this tool on scrap sheer fabric before searing the fringe for your flower. It takes very little time or effort on your part to shrivel the entire fabric patch into charcoal! Just a little curl on the edge is sufficient. Searing will curl the edges of the sheer fabric, giving it a ruffled look.

Layer the organza circles together with the larger circle on the bottom. Position the ruffled circles in the center of the flower and pin in place. The fringe can be free-stitched in place with only a few quilting lines. Do not quilt too much or you will lose dimension.

You may use a heat tool to sear the fringe edges.

Layer the smaller violet circle fringe on top of the black.

The flower center

The poppy center is an egg-shaped patch with a finished size of about 2¼". I faced the entire center shape and turned it inside out through a center slit in the facing. I used a lime-colored fabric for both the front surface and the facing.

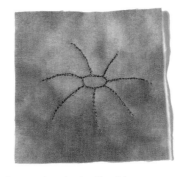

Free-motion the details of the poppy center on the sandwich.

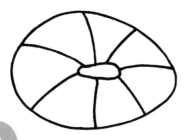

The finished center is ready to arrange on the flower.

Cut a pleasing egg-shaped flower center about 2⅜" x 1⅝" in diameter from freezer paper. Cut improvisationally. Set aside. Cut out a 4" square of fabric for the flower center. Make a sandwich with a 4" square of Pellon™ stabilizer on the bottom, a 4" square of light batting or cotton flannel in the middle and the flower center fabric, right side up, as the top layer. Free-motion stitch the details of the poppy center into the center of the square. If you are not comfortable stitching improvisationally, then first lightly mark the lines of the poppy center with a fabric pencil. Keep the detail area small and concise as you stitch. Limit the stitching to an area about 3" in diameter.

Cut a 4" square of facing fabric and place it on top on the stitched sandwich, right sides together. Carefully align the egg-shaped freezer paper template to the wrong side of the facing fabric. Match up the template's position with the stitching detail of the flower center beneath it. When the freezer paper center is positioned, press the template to the facing and pin the sandwich together. Stitch around the perimeter of the freezer paper egg. Trim excess seam allowance. Make a small slit in the facing, turn inside out, straighten the seam and press. Place the flower center in the fringe/flower center and pin. Attach the center to the flower with a machine blind hemstitch, stitching around the center perimeter with matching thread.

Once positioned, blind hemstitch around the perimeter of the poppy center to lock it in place on the flower.

As you explore dimension and manipulations in this chapter, create freely as in a young child's play. Do not begin a project with a preconceived idea of how the finished project should look. Instead, relax and stay open-minded and flexible. Let your artistry unfold gently. Let the quilt evolve on its own terms and become what it wants to be. The possibilities using the techniques in these pages are boundless. The quilts are waiting only for your hands and imagination to bring them into being.

Engulfed (detail)

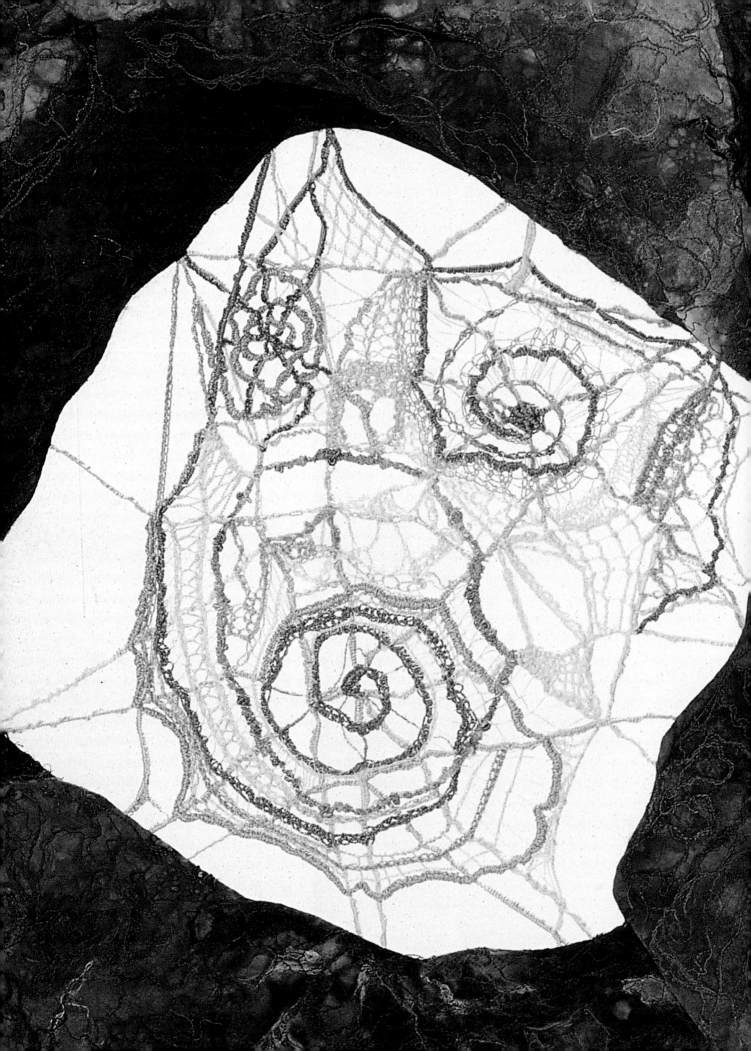

6 New explorations: making openings in your quilts

Left, **The Spider's Web**, *detail.*
Above, **The Spider's Web**. *To better define the latticework, the quilt's opening is shown with a white background.*

English Ivy

To create a very unique quilt that will dazzle all your friends, you may incorporate openwork in your quilt design. Use my easy *English Ivy* pattern to learn how to construct quilts with openings.

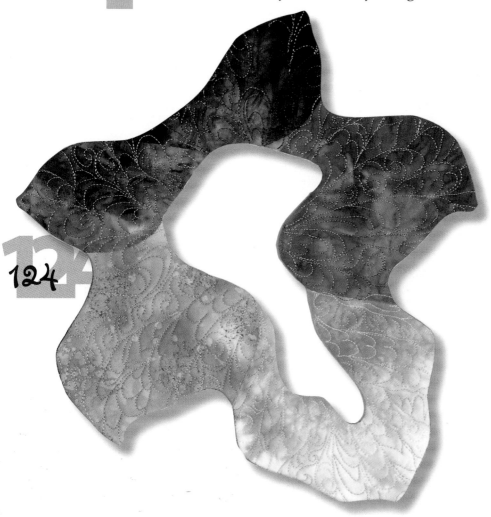

*Pattern for **English Ivy** on page 106.*

The procedure for constructing quilts with openings uses the same technique you've already learned in Chapter 3. The only difference you'll encounter is that any seam allowance lying along the perimeter of the opening must be turned under, thus altering the way you determine the sequence of constructing the templates.

As a reminder and to clarify the terms I use in this chapter:

- **Perimeter** refers to the boundary line or the outside edge. In this chapter it may refer either to the edge of the opening (hole) in the quilt top or to the outer edge (boundary line) of the quilt.

- **Concave curves** are valley curves.

- **Convex curves** are mountain curves.

Supplies:

- two pieces of stabilizer, 20" x 20"

- one piece of batting, 20" x 20"

- assorted scraps for leaf patches

Follow these step-by-step directions:

1 Trace the *English Ivy* master pattern and all the markings as outlined on page 43 onto the dull side of freezer paper. Template 1 is the opening (or hole) in this pattern. Set the master pattern aside.

2 Center the freezer paper tracing on a piece of stabilizer and attach it securely with straight pins. Do not place pins in Template 1.

3 With pattern face up on table, cut out only freezer paper Template 1 on the drawn seam line and discard. Turn pattern over so that stabilizer is now face up. The hole you cut in the freezer paper is shadowed through the stabilizer. Using the shape and edges of the hole as a guide, cut a corresponding, but slightly enlarged, opening in the stabilizer.

The opening in the stabilizer should be about ⅛" larger all around the perimeter of the freezer paper edge. Take care not to cut into the freezer paper pattern as you cut the opening in the stabilizer.

4 Beginning with Template 2, cut the freezer paper template from the pattern and iron it, shiny side down, to the right side of the fabric. Cut patch from the fabric, leaving generous (1") seam allowances (as protection from shrinkage from quilting) along outside boundary lines and approximately ⅜" along all other edges. Clip valley curves in the seam allowance.

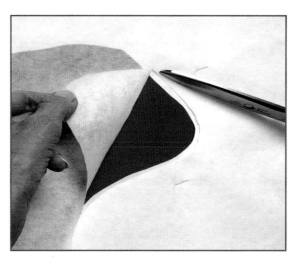

Cut the opening in the stabilizer approximately ⅛" larger than the hole in the freezer paper.

125

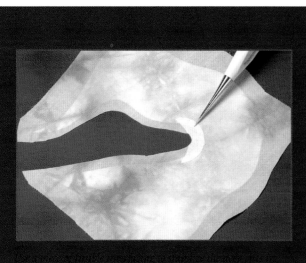

Use a piece of fusible interfacing to stabilize the deep cuts in fabric seam allowances of sharp curves.

*N*ote

Whenever you need to clip a particularly sharp valley curve (such as the curve in Template 2) or have a "V" cut in a patch, you should press a small square of fusible interfacing to the wrong side of the seam allowance fabric. Position the interfacing at the curve so it straddles the seam allowance fabric and extends into the body of the patch. This stabilizes the fibers in the fabric and prevents fraying on heavily clipped or deep cuts on curves.

5 Turn under the seam allowance on the edge marked with arrows and press the fold with a hot steam iron. Return the patch to its place in the design, matching the cut paper edges. The unturned fabric seam allowances should lie between the remaining pinned freezer paper design and the stabilizer. The turned under seam allowance of Patch 2 should lay on top of the stabilizer foundation along the perimeter of the opening, with the crease extending slightly over the cut edge of the stabilizer and into the opening.

Loosen and slowly remove freezer paper, pinning fabric patch in place on the stabilizer as you do so.

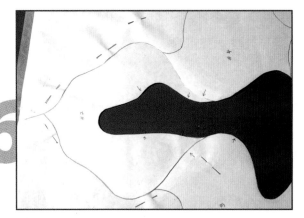

Reposition Template 2 to its place in the pattern.

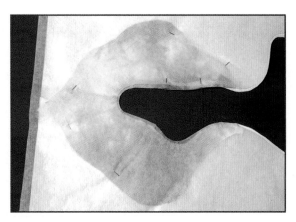

The fabric seam allowance should overlap the opening in the stabilizer.

6 Continue piecing all remaining templates in numerical sequence. Tuck under any protruding fabric tails so they lie beneath succeeding patches. Once several patches are pinned in place and you are satisfied with your fabric and color choices, use fusible web to tack down the turned seam allowances that lay on the opening's perimeter to the stabilizer.

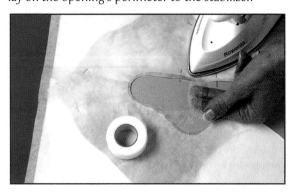

Use Stitch Witchery™ to tack the seam allowance at intervals around the opening. This keeps the template in place until you are ready to finish the quilt.

Tacking ensures the allowance stays securely fixed in place until you are ready to finish the quilt. Turn over the quilt top so that the surface fabric is down, the stabilizer is facing up. Insert a small wedge or bit of fusible web from a roll of Stitch Witchery™ between the seam allowance fabric and the stabilizer. Press with the tip of an iron to fuse. Tack down the seam allowance to the stabilizer at about 2" intervals around the circumference of the opening.

Remove any freezer paper fringes left on the pattern and press well.

Stitching patches near the opening

After completing all 6 patches, sew them in place on the stabilizer foundation using the machine blind hemstitch. Begin by sewing down Patch 3 to Patch 2. Sew from the opening to the outer edges of the quilt top. Lock your beginning stitch in place by putting the sewing machine needle in the fabric seam approximately ⅛" in from the opening.

Bring the bobbin thread to the surface, sew a reverse stitch or two, then sew forward.

I strongly recommend that you stabilize these initial stitches on every seam around the opening by placing a small portion of wax paper on the underside of the quilt top where you start stitching the seam. The piece of wax paper needs to be only large enough to extend part way into the hole and secure the first few stitches of the seams in the body of the patch.

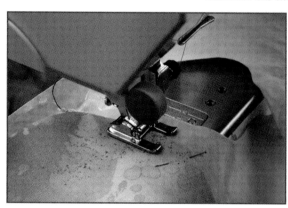

Use a piece of wax paper to stabilize your stitches at the opening.

Using wax paper as a stabilizer keeps the threads from pulling and puckering the fabric at the opening as you begin stitching. The perforated wax paper removes easily once the seam is finished.

Do not stitch around the circumference of the opening. Stitching around the circumference produces ripples along the opening's perimeter and the finished opening will not have a neat ap-

pearance. After all the seams are stitched, snip away the thread tails and press well.

Quilting the quilt top

After the patches are sewn and pressed, sandwich the quilt top and quilt it. The quilt top is the top layer, thin batting is the middle layer and another piece of stabilizer (enlarged if needed) is the bottom layer. There is no backing fabric at this time. Flatten, smooth and pin the layers with safety pins.

Cut a hole in the batting and bottom stabilizer to coincide with the opening in the quilt top. The best way to begin cutting is to work from the front side of the quilt first. Use a pencil to mark the batting, tracing a line around the opening. Then cut out the general shape of the opening on the marked line. For ease during cutting, slightly lift up the edge of quilt top as you cut away the batting/stabilizer. Then flip the quilt to the wrong side and continue trimming the batting and stabilizer backing so the opening in the batting and the stabilizer is ¼" larger than the opening in the quilt top.

As you trim be careful not to cut

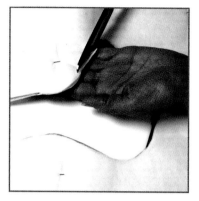

Sandwich the quilt top with stabilizer instead of backing fabric. Make sure the batting and stabilizer on the back are trimmed approximately ¼" from the opening.

the fabric on the quilt top. Use your fingers as a shield between the scissor blade and the fabric seam allowance on underside of the quilt top.

Free-motion or machine quilt as desired, but avoid quilting too heavily at the opening's perimeter. Too much stitching around the opening causes the fabric to pucker and it may also be difficult for you to control your free-motion stitching. If you run off the surface into the opening, don't try to stitch your way back on but stop, cut the threads and resume quilting on the quilt. As you quilt the quilt sandwich, the batting will flatten out and you may need to trim away additional batting. You do not want any batting or stabilizer showing in the opening.

127

Finishing quilt tops with openings

Once you have completed quilting the quilt top, you are ready for the final touches.

1 Using your *English Ivy* master pattern, retrace only the outer edge and the shape of the opening of the leaf on the dull side of a sheet of freezer paper. Cut out the leaf shape and opening on the drawn lines.

2 Position the large template shiny side down on the surface of the quilt top. Match the opening shape and align the rest of the template with the body of the leaf so it is centered.

Cut out the outline of the leaf and position it on the quilt top.

There will be some minor shrinkage of the quilt top due to the quilting. In a small project such as this the amount of shrinkage shouldn't be enough to cause a problem, especially if you left generous outside boundary seam allowances on the fabric patches during the construction process.

3 After the freezer paper template is centered, press it to the quilt top. Set the machine for a long basting stitch. Using a blending thread as the top thread and a brightly colored thread in the bobbin, stitch next to the freezer paper edge and sew around the entire perimeter of the *English Ivy* leaf. Remove the freezer paper template and discard.

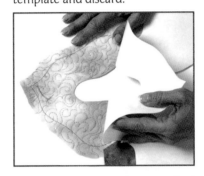

Stitch around the entire perimeter of leaf and remove the paper template.

4 Place a backing fabric that blends well with the leaf color face down on the quilt top surface, right sides together.

Center the backing fabric, right side down, on top of the quilt top.

Smooth, press and safety pin securely. Turn the sandwich over so the stabilizer is face up. You will see the shape of the ivy leaf outlined in brightly colored thread.

5 Reset your machine to a short stitch length. Carefully stitch around the perimeter of the leaf, just barely inside the stitched outline.

Stitch on the back of the quilt, just to the inside of the colored basting outline stitch.

Your goal is to achieve a smooth line of stitching without erratic or jagged stitches. For best results, try to run the line of stitching continuously with smooth motions. Keep the start/stop to a minimum.

6 Trim away excess seam allowance to about ¼" of seam line. Clip valley curves. Gently turn quilt inside out through the opening. Use a point turner or blunt instrument to push out and straighten seams. Press well to flatten quilt.

128

7 To eliminate puffiness and ensure that the backing fabric does not shift while you finish the opening, you may wish to tack the wrong side of the backing fabric to the inside of the quilt top. This step may only be necessary with medium and large quilts. Secure with bits of fusible webbing placed between the backing fabric and quilt top layers. For best results, use the lightest weight webbing available.

If you wish, secure backing to quilt top with bits of webbing.

Tack a small area at a time starting at the farthest areas of the quilt and working your way toward the opening, but do not fuse near the opening yet.

8 Turn the quilt to the right side. Use a fabric pencil to trace the shape of the opening on the wrong side of the backing fabric.

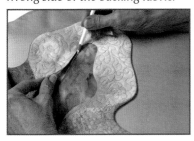

Draw the opening shape on backing fabric.

Iron snippets of woven fusible interfacing to the sharp curves on the inside of the backing fabric before clipping the area to eliminate fraying.

Use a bit of fusible interfacing to reinforce the deep curves cut in the backing fabric and prevent fraying.

9 Make a slit in the backing fabric, being careful not to cut within ½" of the marked line of the opening. Cut out the center fabric of the opening, leaving about ⅜" seam allowance from the drawn line.

Cut out opening leaving a seam allowance. Clip curves.

Clip valley curves in the seam allowance. When first clipping curves in a seam allowance in an opening, don't clip the backing fabric too deep. It is better to clip a little at a time. You can always clip the allowance deeper as needed, but the backing fabric is

difficult to mend once it is cut too deeply.

10 Turn under the seam allowance of the backing fabric along the perimeter of the opening. Match the crease of the backing fabric to the corresponding crease of the patch in the quilt top. You may have to trim off a little more backing fabric or make the clips a little deeper to achieve a perfect match. It is better to take off a little at a time than to cut off too much. When the two edges match, press backing allowance and pin both edges together.

129

Match and align the turned seam allowances from the quilt top and the backing fabric.

Whipstitch the backing to the quilt top. Stitch a circle ring on the back for hanging and add a label.

Alternate method for making openings

As with all things, there is more than one way to accomplish a task. Please note that this technique works best for openings that are valley (curved inward) curves such as circles or ovals, or an asymmetrical opening that is mostly curved inward. This option doesn't work as well with openings containing mountain (outward) curves because it is more difficult to turn the fabric seam allowances for mountain curves over the stabilizer's edge with exact precision. Thus the perimeter of the hole won't be as accurate to the pattern as with the previous technique.

Spring Blossom

Also, there is a difference in how the seam allowance for this alternate method is turned at the opening. With the main technique, the turned seam allowance lies between the surface patches and the stabilizer. A few strategically placed tacks of webbing will keep the allowances locked in place until you sandwich the quilt. With this alternate option the fabric seam allowance lies on the back of the stabilizer and must be well pressed and secured with pieces of webbing to hold it in place. This alternative technique works great with *Spring Blossom*.

I encourage you to try both methods. Decide which one works best and is easiest for you.

Supplies:

- stabilizer (2 pieces), 18" x 24"

- batting and backing fabric, 18" x 24"

- scraps of fabric for petals and leaves.

130

1 The pattern for *Spring Blossom* is on page 167. Trace the *Spring Blossom* pattern and all the markings onto dull side of freezer paper. Template 1 is the opening in this pattern.

2 Attach the freezer paper pattern to the stabilizer with straight pins. Do not place pins in Template 1.

3 Cut out Template 1 from the freezer paper and the stabilizer at the same time on the drawn seam line and discard. Leave the remaining freezer paper pattern and stabilizer intact as you cut the opening.

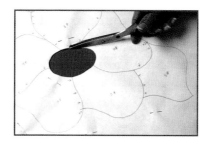

Cut the opening in the pattern and the stabilizer the same size.

4 Begin piecing by cutting out freezer paper Template 2 (a petal). Press it, shiny side down, to the right side of the fabric. Cut patch from fabric with generous 1" seam allowances on the outside boundary line and 3⁄8" along the perimeter of the opening and between the seam lines. Return the patch to the design, matching the cut paper edges. The seam allowance running along the

perimeter of the opening will overlap the opening but remain raw-edged for now. Loosen and slowly remove freezer paper, pinning fabric patch in place on the stabilizer as you do so. Please note that with this technique variation, the patches are sewn down before the seam allowances are turned under at the opening.

5 Continue piecing all remaining templates in numerical sequence. Turn under the seam allowances on edges marked with small arrows, but not along the perimeter of the opening. Tuck under any protruding fabric tails so they lie beneath succeeding patches. Remove any fringes of freezer paper left on pattern/stabilizer and begin sewing down the patches, following the directions on page 126.

Explorations

Add dimension to your blossom petals using contrast between the petals to simulate highlights and shadows. You may wish to use light value/color fabrics denoting a springtime palette for your project. You may need to line some of the lightest pastel patches to prevent shadowing. Please refer to page 45 for instructions on "Lining a patch".

If you line a patch, match the cut edge of the lining with the edge of the opening. The lining should not overlap the opening in the stabilizer. During the construction process the seam allowances of all the patches will overlap the edge of the opening. They will be turned under after the patches are sewn down to the stabilizer.

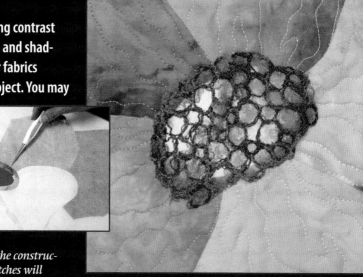

Add dimension to your blossom petals using contrast between the petals to simulate highlights and shadows.

Turning under the seam allowance openings

6 Turn over quilt top with the stabilizer facing up. You will see that the seam allowances from the surface patches extend beyond the perimeter of the opening in the stabilizer. Clip all the valley curves almost to the edge of the stabilizer.

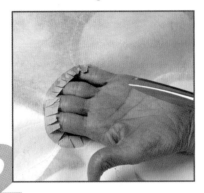

Clip the curves of the seam allowance almost to the edge of the stabilizer.

Flip the quilt top over and working from the top surface, fold the seam allowances over the edge of the opening to the back of the quilt top, pressing the allowances with hot steam iron as you go.

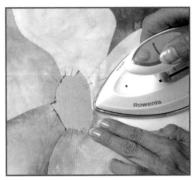

Turn under the seam allowance, matching the edge of the opening in the stabilizer.

Try to follow the shape of the opening's outline as accurately as possible. As you turn the seam allowance you may find it easier to work from the wrong side of the quilt top rather than the front surface. Use the method that works best for you.

7 To ensure that the turned allowances around the circumference of the opening stay securely fixed in place, you should tack down the allowances at close intervals. To do this, insert a small wedge or bit of fusible web from a roll of Stitch Witchery™ between the seam allowance fabric and the stabilizer. Press with an iron to fuse.

Sandwich and quilt *Spring Blossom* as directed on page 127, "Quilting the Quilt Top". To finish the quilt, follow the directions on page 128 "Finishing quilt tops with openings" using the *Spring Blossom* master pattern outline instead of *English Ivy* in Step 1.

132

Explorations

1 The backing fabric may be left intact (uncut) during finishing process, and an open, lacy latticework may be inserted in the opening, lying between the quilt top and backing fabric, allowing the backing fabric to show through.

2 Combine two techniques to make an improvisational block quilt (Chapter 4) with openings. Make the center patch in the block larger in size and use the random improvisational technique (page 133) to make the opening.

Random improvisational openings

The previous two techniques involved making an opening in a quilt top containing multiple patches and fabrics. There may be times you want to insert a random opening into a single piece of fabric. This is an informal, freeing and simple technique perfect for improvisational design.

Cut a shape from fusible webbing and fuse it to the wrong side of the fabric. Remove the protective paper. Staying within the margins of the fused webbing (about ½" from the edge on all sides), cut out a smaller version of the same shape from the fabric. Again, keeping within the boundaries of the fused webbing, clip the valley curves or corners. Turn the fabric to the right side and turn under the seam allowances on all sides of the opening. Be sure the creases are smooth with no raw edges showing. Using a sheet of parchment paper beneath the fabric to protect the ironing surface, press to fuse the seam allowance.

Fuse the shape on the wrong side of the fabric.

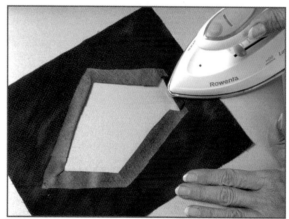

Cut a smaller version of the shape within the margins of the fusible web. Clip curves or corners, turn under all the seam allowances and press.

133

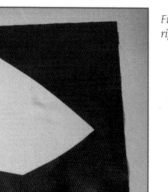

Finished opening., right-side up.

Working with holes in your own design

Now that you have completed the *English Ivy* and *Spring Blossom* patterns, you may wish to try adding one or several holes into your own designs. Here are a few hints and suggestions to help you as you explore and plan your project.

Choosing where to put the opening

Once you decide to incorporate openings into your work and are in the process of drafting the design for the quilt, here are some thoughts to consider:

- Where will opening placement in the design deliver the best visual impact?

- Where will it best enhance the quilt?

- Are the openings balanced throughout the surface of the quilt design?

- Where will the opening be the least difficult to construct?

- Will the hanging rod show in the opening? This is an important point to consider and you should plan for the hanging sleeve as you decide where to place your openings in the design. Keep in mind that the hanging sleeve does not have to stretch the entire width of the quilt top. See page 164.

The hanging sleeve can be constructed in segments and staggered on the back of the quilt to accommodate the openings. This the back of Summer's Bounty.

You can divide the sleeve into small segments. Plan to position each sleeve segment between openings and at least 2-3" higher than the topmost opening in the quilt. Thus, you need to plan for at least a 2-3" clearance area above the highest opening to accommodate the hanging rod so it doesn't show when you hang the quilt.

Generally you should designate a patch from the background to be the hole, rather than a patch that is part of the focal point. However, as is the case with all the rules of art, you can bend or break the rules to accomplish your goal! For instance, a supplementary leaf in a floral design can be earmarked as an opening and a web or latticework of threads encased within the opening for visual excitement.

For a description of adding latticework to openings, refer to page 137.

The technique of incorporating openings in your quilt is best suited to small and medium size quilts, especially while learning the technique. Keep in mind that when the finished quilt hangs, the color of the wall or drape behind it will show through the openings and influence the visual impact of the quilt. This consideration may alter your fabric color choices as you complete the work.

134

After you decide which templates will be openings in the quilt, take a look at the shape of each hole. If the shape has an acute inside corner, modify the sharpness by rounding out the angle.

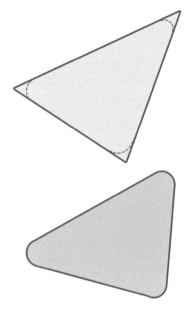

Modify the deep V's in a design by rounding the curves. It will be easier to construct and will not substantially impact the look of the design.

You should be able to change the line minimally without compromising your design. This simple adjustment will make the final stages of the construction process much easier for you as you fold under and stitch the quilt backing to the quilt surface.

Numbering sequence for the design.

When planning the numerical sequence for your design you must remember that any seam allowance of a patch touching the edge of an opening must be turned under. Therefore, all templates surrounding the opening will have an edge turned under and you will be working from the opening (center) outwards when determining layering sequence.

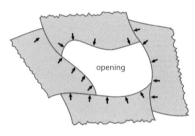

The raw seam allowance of any patch touching the edge of the opening must be turned under. Mark the template edges with small arrows.

If you have multiple openings in your pattern, a fabric patch that sits between two openings will have two or even three sides turned under. Remember to mark the seams to be turned under with small arrows on each template. In some cases you may need to splice seams or reverse sequence direction to continue or cover sharp points.

Please refer to page 69 for guidelines for splicing seams.

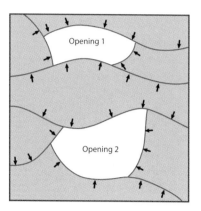

If a patch lies between two openings, both sides of the patch must be turned under.

Construction hints

• For oversized designs, see page 50 to enlarge stabilizer.

• Start the piecing process at one of the designed openings. Usually beginning at an opening somewhere near the center of the quilt is best. Even though you may have several openings intended for your design, cut out and work on only one at a time. As the construction progresses you may change your mind about placement for an opening. Complete 4-6 templates before stitching. Press well and resume the piecing sequence on the quilt surface with the next set of 4-6 templates. As your quilt top progresses, you may decide to incorporate more openings. At that point in construction, you can determine which seam allowances should be turned under.

Finishing quilt tops with multiple openings

1 Once you have completed quilting the quilt top and are ready for the finish you must determine the final shape of the quilt. You may decide that you want to alter or modify the outside perimeter of the quilt from your original pattern design. Mark your final binding line with a fabric pencil and flexible curve if needed (refer to page 155). Thread your machine with a color of thread that blends with the colors on the quilt top and a brightly colored thread in the bobbin. Using a basting stitch, sew along your binding line on the surface of your quilt top. The bright bobbin thread will be visible on the stabilizer back.

2 Press your backing fabric and place it right side up on a table. If possible, use clamps to stretch the backing fabric taut but not distorted. Center your quilt top, right side down, on the backing fabric. Pin with safety pins.

3 Stitch the quilt together, stabilizer side up, following the brightly colored bobbin line. Sew around the entire perimeter, keeping a smooth stitching line. Trim the seam allowance to ⅜" from the stitching line. Clip valley curves.

4 Choose the largest opening in the quilt and gently turn the entire quilt inside out through the opening. Use a point turner or blunt instrument to smooth out the seams and press well. You may want to tack the backing fabric to the quilt top so the backing fabric does not shift while you are finishing multiple openings. If so, use bits of a lightweight fusible webbing to secure. Tack small areas at a time, starting at remote areas of the quilt and working your way toward the openings, but do not fuse near the openings yet.

5 Trace the shape of the opening on the backing fabric with a marking pencil. Make a slit in the backing fabric, being careful not to cut within ½" of the marking line. *Cut and process only one opening at a time.* Tack with additional fusible web if needed to prevent shifting of backing fabric.

6 Carefully cut out the center fabric of the opening, leaving about ½" seam allowance from the drawn line. For sharp or deep curves press small patches of fusible interfacing on the inside of the backing fabric before clipping them to eliminate fraying. Turn seam allowance of the backing fabric to the inside, matching its crease to the edge of the opening of the quilt top. When the two edges match, press backing allowance and pin both edges together.

7 Turn and pin the seams of all of the openings. Press the backing fabric to be sure the fabric lies smoothly and without wrinkles, especially between openings. If the backing fabric does not lie flat between the openings, readjust the seams and repin the fabric. Hand whipstitch the crease of the turned-under backing fabric to the crease of patches on the quilt's top surface.

8 Add hanging sleeve and label. Use level and mark straight lines on the back with fabric pencil for sleeve placement.

Latticework

Once you become experienced in making openings in your quilt, you may choose the option of adding an open, lacy latticework of threads, yarns and fibers in these openings.

Latticework may consists of threads, yarns and/or fabric manipulations such as pleats or tubes. The threads are stitched onto a water-soluble stabilizer such as Aqua Mesh™. For instructions on making tubes and pleats see Chapter 5, "Exploring Dimension." After the stitching is complete, the water-soluble stabilizer is immersed in water, dissolving the stabilizer and leaving a web of thread, yarns and fabric intact. Once dried, the latticework can be inserted into your quilts.

There are several ways to use the latticework.

Latticework that lies partially on top of the quilt, bridging an opening, or one that is sandwiched between an opening with fabric in back of it, has sufficient support for the threads in the web. In these instances the latticework is stitched using only the water-soluble stabilizer, immersed, dried and inserted directly to the quilt top.

1 Position the latticework on top of the quilt, allowing it to bridge the opening. *Spring Blossom*, detail.

2 Sandwich the latticework between the quilt top and a backing fabric or layer, allowing it to cover the open space. The backing fabric will be visible through the latticework.

3 Sandwich the latticework between the quilt top and backing fabric, positioning it so it spans the opening. *Windows*, detail.

Latticework bridging openings

Even though the latticework comprising the center of *Spring Blossom* extends across the opening of the flower, it also lies partially on the quilt top, giving the threads some support. Before the latticework flower center is added, the quilt is completely finished and the backing is hand-stitched to the quilt top at the opening.

All threads used to stitch the lattice will be visible once the stabilizer is washed away. Choose a thread for the bobbin that complements or enhances the top threads you are using. This is a great time to use heavy decorative threads too thick to pass through a sewing machine needle and generally reserved for couching or bobbin drawing or sewing. I usually thread my machine with two or more threads on the top.

Be aware that when creating latticework for openings, the more threads you use and the more interconnected they are with each other, the more stable the latticework will be. Most of the time I free-motion the latticework heavily with threads and meandering stitches to connect all the components together to create a dense but see-through machine lace or web.

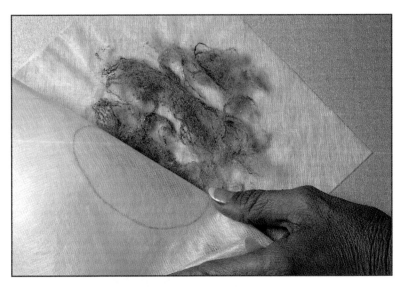

Arrange yarns, wool or threads to lie between two sheets of water-soluble stabilizer.

To make a flower center of stitched threads, you need only some water-soluble stabilizer, decorative threads and yarns. For the center of this quilt I had some alpaca fleece on hand that I'd found at a show and decided it was perfect to include in the flower center to give it texture and interest.

To make a flower center such as the center for *Spring Blossom*:

1 Measure the dimensions of the hole and add 5" to each dimension. Cut two pieces of water-soluble stabilizer in those dimensions (length + 5" and width + 5"). Lay the water-soluble stabilizer on a flat surface and center the opening of the quilt on top of it. Trace the shape of the quilt opening onto the stabilizer with a pencil. This will give you an idea how large the center needs to be while you are stitching the web. You

should have at least three inches allowance on each side of the marked line of the opening.

2 Arrange yarns, snippets of fabric confetti, wool, threads, ribbons, glitzy fibers or other materials so they lie between the sheets of the water-soluble stabilizer in the general area of the traced opening. The materials should extend beyond the traced opening at least 1". If working with lots of tiny snippets or bits of confetti, use two pieces of tulle to trap and keep them in place after the water-soluble stabilizer is dissolved.

138

For the flower center for *Spring Blossom*, I stitched heavily in a circular motion using free-motion and an open-toe darning foot, varying the size of the circles and leaving the center of the circles untouched for a puffy look.

3 Once the creative stitching is complete, dip the water-soluble latticework in warm water and soak for a few minutes until the stabilizer melts away. Gently rinse the lattice with clean water sev-

4 Arrange the flower center on top of the quilt top so it is centered across the opening, but still lies partially on the quilt top. Pin in place. The latticework can be stitched on the quilt top either by hand or by machine. If you use a machine, use a straight stitch to sew around the outer edge of the flower center. If stitching by machine, the bobbin thread will show on the back. Use matching thread for both the top and bobbin thread.

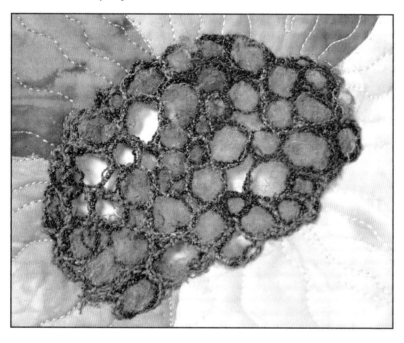

Extend the stitching for the flower center at least an inch beyond the traced marking. You will need extra latticework on all sides to bridge the opening and to attach it to the quilt top. There may also be some shrinkage in the latticework during the immersion process. In addition, stitch heavily around the outside perimeter to create a finished "edge" for the flower center. For interest, make the outside shape of the flower center irregular, not perfectly round or oval.

eral times or until the stickiness is gone. Pick up the latticework carefully with both hands and place on a terry towel. Pat dry. Cover the latticework with a thin cotton press cloth and iron gently. Do not use paper towels or terrycloth as a press cloth. Allow to dry completely.

139

Latticework spanning openings between the quilt top and backing

If the latticework spans an opening, especially a large opening, and lies between the quilt top and backing, you need a little more support for the threads and yarn. Therefore, in addition to using water-soluble stabilizer, I connect the manipulations and threads to a permanent "frame" of heavyweight Pellon™ stabilizer. The stabilizer ensures the finished lattice is the proper size and the threads and/or manipulations are positioned the way I want them. Using a frame also help gives even support to the latticework and locks the threads in place at the edges of the opening, assuring the threads will stay embedded in the quilt body and not work their way loose. The lattice/frame is inserted between the backing fabric and the quilt top just before the front and back of the opening are hand stitched together.

Before starting the lattice, complete the quilt top with the opening, sandwich it with batting and use Pellon™ stabilizer instead of a backing fabric. Quilt the quilt as desired before proceeding to the next step.

1 Place the quilted quilt face up on a table or design wall. Working on one opening at a time, cut, position and pin a piece of Pellon™ stabilizer in back of the opening in the quilt top. Cut the stabilizer so that it is large enough to extend about five inches beyond the opening on all sides. The extra amount of stabilizer allowed for the latticework's frame in this step will give the latticework stability during construction; otherwise

2 Trace the shape of the quilt opening onto stabilizer with a pencil. Make a pencil notation on the stabilizer indicating which side is top/front. You'll be surprised how easy it is to become confused without these notations! Remove the stabilizer from the back of the quilt. Using the traced shape as a general guideline, cut out the opening's shape enlarging its size and perimeter an additional inch all the way around. The cut does

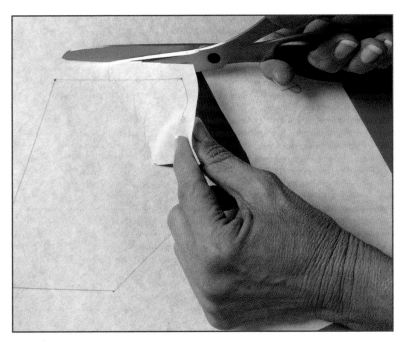

Using the traced shape as a guide, cut out the opening's shape enlarging its size and perimeter an additional inch all the way around.

the frame can easily become misshapen or puckered. The excess stabilizer will be trimmed away later after the threads and manipulations are securely attached.

not have to match perfectly with the actual tracing. The additional opening space gives you room for error, shrinkage and assurance that the stabilizer won't be visible when it is encased between the quilt top and the backing.

140

3 Cut two pieces of water-soluble stabilizer. These sheets do not need to be as large as the Pellon™ stabilizer, but they should be large enough to overlap the hole in the Pellon™ by at least 1½ to 2". Place one sheet of water-soluble stabilizer underneath the Pellon™ frame and another sheet on top of the Pellon™ frame. The bottom layer of water-soluble stabilizer ensures the sandwich slides smoothly through the sewing machine without getting caught on the edges of the Pellon™ frame. The cottony textured surface of the Aqua Mesh™ helps to grip and hold the threads in place on the top layer. Be sure that all three layers are lying flat and smooth. Pin or machine baste around the perimeter of the opening to secure the three stabilizers.

At this point, you must make a decision about what contents to include in the latticework for your quilt. You may create the lattice-work at whim, including decorative threads and yarns at random. If you want a particular effect or have a more controlled, structured lattice in mind, you can proceed with this next step.

On the water-soluble stabilizer, mark the exact point where you want pleats or yarns to extend into the opening.

Reposition and pin the stabilizer sandwich in back of the quilt top on your design wall, centering it so the Pellon™ frame aligns and lies evenly around the opening. You can extend some of the elements already in the quilt top such as straight or pleated tubes so they appear to continue into the opening.

You can use a pencil to mark the exact spot on the water-soluble stabilizer where you want threads to fall, thread color preferences, etc. Refer to Chapter 5 for directions on making tubes and pleats.

Lightweight fabric manipulations such as small to medium tubes do quite well in a latticework opening. You should always use tubes so the open latticework looks finished from either the front or back of the quilt. The tubes can extend straight across the opening, or they can be twisted or pleated. Simply fold or turn the pleats as you want them to appear and pin them to the water-soluble stabilizer. Please be sure that both ends of a tube and any lines of stitching spanning the opening overlap onto the Pellon™ frame and are secured there with a locking stitch.

Stitching latticework

For this type of latticework, I usually use a straight or decorative stitch and a regular presser foot. Stitch down the pleats, beginning and ending the line of stitching by locking the fabric ends to the Pellon™ stabilizer.

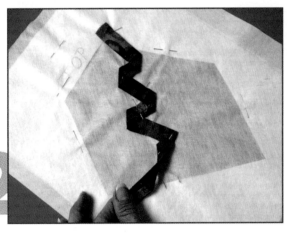

Arrange and pin the pleats on the water-soluble stabilizer. Secure with lines of stitching.

Make the locking stitches about ½" from the edge of the stabilizer. You can stitch on the fabric tube in either straight or wavy lines, but depending on the width of the manipulation, I recommend that you make at least two or three lines of stitching through the manipulation to secure it in the latticework.

You can also stitch and couch yarns, perle cotton thread, and other decorative threads from one side of the opening to the other, again securing the thread on each side of the Pellon™ frame. You can incorporate wool, fabric or ribbon snippets in the web, creating a distinctive look for your latticework.

When creating latticework to span an opening, the more threads you use and the more interconnected they are with each other, the more stable the latticework will be. If your lattice consists of only a few criss-crossing threads, there won't be enough support and the threads may sag. Do not stitch wavy lines unless you support them with plenty of crisscrossing and interconnecting threads. Once the water-soluble stabilizer is removed, what started out as the perfect looking wavy line when stitched on stabilizer is now drooping in swags. Keep an open mind. Even in nature the threads within a spider's web swag. In some cases, this look can be a fun and interesting effect for the lattice; it just won't be what you anticipated.

You can use some of the decorative stitches on your machine for unusual effects in the latticework. If you decide to use a decorative stitch, it is very important to stabilize the stitch by first stitching down several lines of straight stitching across the opening to provide support for the decorative stitch. This step keeps the thread in the decorative stitch intact once the water-soluble stabilizer is removed. No matter how tight or dense a decorative stitched line appears to be, without the lines of straight stitching to support it, the decorative stitching will unravel and stretch once the water-soluble stabilizer is gone.

142

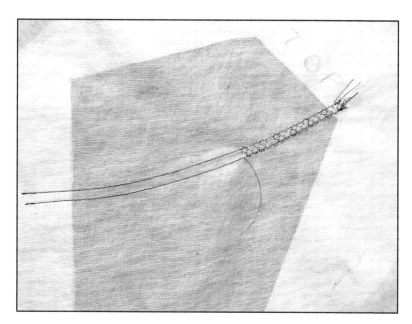

Span parallel lines of stitching across the opening to support wide decorative stitches.

Set your machine on a small length straight stitch; use regular thread in an appropriate color. Stitch back and forth across the opening. Make at least three lines of stitching, four if you are sewing with a dense or wide decorative stitch.

For narrow decorative stitches, the supporting lines of stitching can be sewn directly on top of each other. To support wider decorative stitches, make two double lines of stitching about ⅛" apart. In both cases, be sure the decorative stitch is centered on top of the supporting lines of thread. Lock the beginning and end stitches on the Pellon™ stabilizer. Again, be sure to support these threads even more by interconnecting them many times with other threads or manipulations for ultimate support.

If a thread in the lattice sags, you can tighten it by pulling the excess to the Pellon™ stabilizer frame and securing it by stitching over the thread several times. You can also interweave additional threads back and forth by hand through the sagging thread to take up the slack.

In my quilts, I used only fabric in the tube manipulations for latticework and it was strong enough to hold steady without sagging. If you do experience some slack you certainly could stabilize the wrong side of the tube fabric with fusible interfacing for extra support in the openings.

Once the lattice is complete, process it by immersing in water, drying and pressing it flat. Allow it to dry completely. Trim away any excess thread tails and bulk from any fabric manipulations, but *do not cut the stabilizer frame yet.*

Inserting latticework in an opening

For the easiest and most polished appearance, follow this method for inserting latticework into your quilt. Use the envelope finish to back the quilted quilt top (page 156). Cut the opening out of the backing fabric and turn under the backing fabric seams as directed on page 129. The quilt should be completed with a backing fabric and the backing fabric turned under and pinned at the openings. The latticework is then inserted into the opening between the quilt top and backing fabric as the last step before hand-stitching the front and back of the opening together. By working in this sequence you have the visual advantage of seeing clearly as you turn under the backing fabric's seam allowances along the opening's perimeters. You can match the backing to the quilt top with precision and without interference from the manipulations or threads in the latticework.

The procedure

1 Proceed to finish the quilted quilt top with an envelope backing and turn the quilt inside out through the opening. Cut out the opening from the backing fabric, leaving seam allowances and clip valley curves. Flip the quilt over to the back and turn under the seam allowances along the open-

ing perimeter so the allowance crease matches to the crease from the quilt top and pin. Press the backing well to set the creases. Set quilt aside.

2 Trim the outside edge of the lattice/Pellon™ stabilizer to about 1½" around the opening, creating a narrow stabilizer frame around the lattice. If the stabilizer is not lying flat and evenly, press again.

3 With the top side of the latticework facing up, use fusible webbing from a roll to outline the entire perimeter of the opening.

Outline the Pellon™ stabilizer frame with fusible webbing.

Place the webbing close to the perimeter.

4 Cut an ample sheet of parchment paper to use as a press cloth. Cut the parchment paper large enough to protect your iron and quilt top in the area you are working. The fusible webbing will not stick to the parchment paper and you can reuse the same paper numerous times. Cover the webbing with the parchment paper and press to fuse the webbing to the stabilizer. Work in short lengths or process one side at a time rather

than outlining the entire opening at once. If you are fusing webbing to a narrow area or strip of stabilizer, use the parchment paper beneath the stabilizer as well to protect your ironing board. The fusing will help to not only secure the threads, but also to bond the latticework to the back of the quilt top once the lattice is inserted.

5 Unpin the seam allowance at the opening on the quilt. Place your quilt on a flat surface right side up. Carefully insert the lattice, slipping it between the backing fabric and the quilt top.

Insert the lattice in the opening between the backing fabric and the stabilizer on the back of the quilt surface. The fusible webbing on the lattice's Pellon™ frame should face the stabilizer on the quilt.

The fusing on the lattice's frame should face the Pellon™ stabilizer on the back of the quilt top. Adjust the lattice so the threads and its stabilizer frame lie flat and evenly between the two layers. The frame and threads should be extended and taut but not stretched. Be sure no stabilizer from the frame shows in the opening. When the lattice is positioned correctly, lightly pin for a temporary hold and flip the quilt

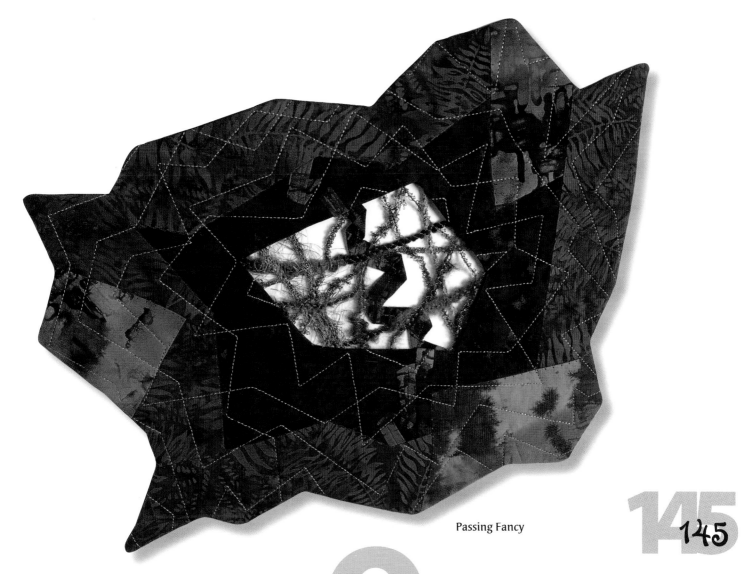
Passing Fancy

over. Readjust the seam allowances of the backing fabric to perfectly match the creases of the seams on the quilt top and pin securely. Once the pins are in place and the lattice looks satisfactory, press the backing fabric. This will adhere the lattice's frame to the back of the quilt top.

6 After all the latticework is inserted in the openings and the seams properly adjusted, press the back again to smooth and even up the backing fabric. Readjust the pins if the backing fabric does not lie smoothly between openings. Whipstitch the backing to the quilt top by hand, using a thread that matches the backing fabric color. Pay special attention to the corners of the openings. Reinforce the narrow seam allowances in deep V corners with a couple of extra stitches. As you hand-stitch along the edge of the openings, run the needle through the fabric manipulations and threads as well to reinforce the lattice.

Only your imagination is the limit as you design quilts. There are endless possibilities for using openings and latticework in your quilting and fiber art. The unusual shapes and visual effects these techniques produce will help define your unique style and set you apart from the crowd. Have fun as you use these methods to explore your potential and let your creativity take flight.

7 Improvisational borders, finishes & bindings

Whether you constructed your quilt top using freezer paper templates as you did with the *My Star Dances* pattern (Chapter 3) or with an improvisational method, you may continue to add more design interest to the quilt top by using improvisational borders. As with other improvisational concepts, you are limited only by your imagination when designing creative border ideas.

Left, **Rhapsody in Pink**, *detail.*
Above, **Rhapsody in Pink**.

An improvisational border may be as simple as the process of turning under the seam allowances of straight-edged strips of fabric and applying one strip per side to the quilt top. Another option is to overlap strips at different angles to create wedges. Other border ideas may include cutting fabric at random into a strip or patch with a freeform curvy line or drafting a simple freezer paper template for a scalloped border. Begin this chapter with an untrimmed quilt top in hand and a desire to explore exciting new finishing techniques.

148

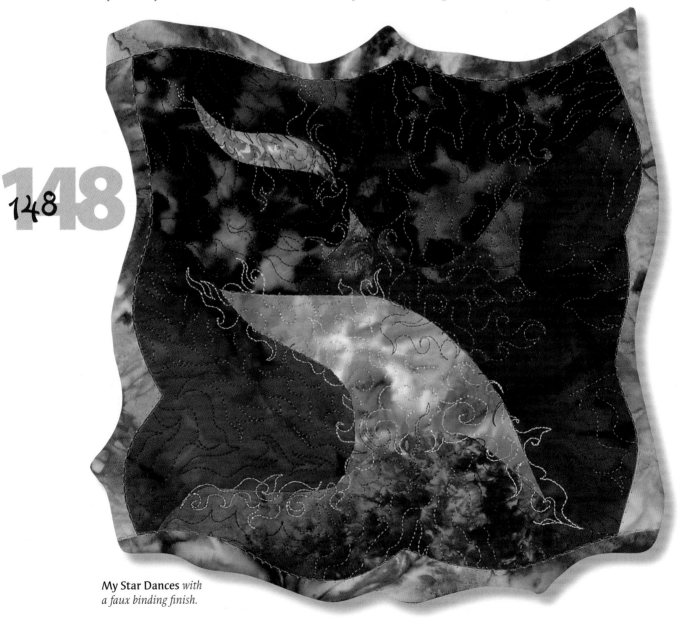

My Star Dances *with a faux binding finish.*

$\mathcal{B}$order Options

Impromptu straight borders

To add a **straight** border to a quilt top, cut each strip as long as the length (or width) of the quilt top plus an additional 3" on each end of the strip (length + 6"). The extra strip length allows for overlapping adjoining borders, perpendicular border strips and mitering corners (page 152). Working from the right side of the fabric, simply turn under a ⅜"-½" seam allowance on the top edge of the strip to the back. Position the creased edge of the first border strip on top of the quilt as desired, overlapping any raw edges and pin in place. When the border strips for all four sides are constructed and arranged to your liking, use a machine blind hemstitch and blending thread color to sew them in place.

For a straight border simply turn under the seam allowance on a strip and position it on the quilt top.

Curved and scalloped borders

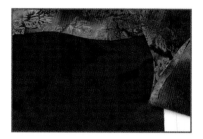

For a curved border, clip curves and position.

You may make your quilt unique by sculpting random **curves** into the top edge of the straight border strip, clipping valley curves before turning under the seam allowance. If you want to adhere to a definite design pattern, design and draw the border templates on freezer paper first. Use the paper templates as a guide and construct the border strips using the basic technique you learned in Chapter 3. The size of the border strips should be at least 3" wide.

Use a flexible curve to design a **scalloped** border and draw gentle swags on freezer paper. Vary the size of the curved arcs. Rather than designing the border from corner to corner on each side of the quilt top, I find that creating a border that begins at

the middle of one side of the quilt top, curves around the corner and extends to the middle of the adjoining side of the quilt top results in a neater, more pleasing appearance.

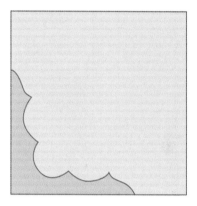

To make scalloped borders, draft a template to extend from side to side of the quilt top, rather than corner to corner. Many times, the freezer paper template can be reversed, slightly revised or simply reused as is for other sides of the quilt top.

Cabbage Rose

Pink Tulip. *A wedged border is two straight strips—one overlapping the other and positioned at an angle.*

Wedged borders

The wedged border is a fast and simple, yet effective, border treatment. The borders will be applied on the quilt top one side at a time. Use two strips of fabric as the border patches for each side of the design. The bottom border strip is applied first and lies directly on the quilt top. It is usually a color that is part of the focal point. For instance, if the star in *My Star Dances* pattern is orange, you might consider using a hue of orange, either the same color, lighter or darker orange for the bottom border strip. In *Pink Tulip* I chose pink for the wedged borders to enhance the flower.

The second or top strip will overlap the bottom strip at an angle, creating a narrow wedge. The top strip must be of a different, contrasting fabric, perhaps a fabric or color used in the background of the star pattern. The contrast between the two fabrics will create the shape of a wedge in the color of the focal point. The size of the wedge can be as narrow or wide as you like. Even the narrowest slice of the focal point color in the wedge will go a long way to enhance the main focus—the star. As a word of caution, don't make the focal colored wedges in the border so wide or full of color that they detract rather than enhance the focus. Use your judgment.

Here are the instructions for wedged borders:

1 Make a bottom border patch by cutting a strip of fabric in a hue or the same color as the focal point of the design. The width of the strip can be about 2", but the length depends on how long you want the wedge to be. To be effective and visually interesting, vary the length of the wedges on each side of the design.

2 Press the strip smooth and turn under approximately ½" straight seam allowance along the top edge of the strip. Press the allowance to set the crease. Position the patch on the design at random in the area where you wish the border to be in the design. Pin in place on the quilt top.

3 Choose a contrasting fabric for the second strip. Cut the strip approximately 3" wide and as long as the length of the design plus an additional 3" on each end of the strip (length +6") if you plan to miter the borders. Turn under a ½" seam allowance along the top edge of the strip and press to set the crease. Position the second strip so it overlaps the first strip at an angle, creating a wedge.

4 Construct and pin the border patches on all sides of the design before you stitch. It is likely you will change, readjust and interweave the patches as you work on the border design. Once you are satisfied with the border results, stitch the patches in place using a machine blind hemstitch and matching or blending thread. Begin by stitching down the bottom patches first. Press well. Finish using an envelope or faced binding.

Explorations

1 Either or both wedge strips may be sculpted into a curvy edge. Clip curves and turn under the seam allowance as usual.

For an unusual border treatment, add curves to the wedge.

2 Either strip may be positioned at a skewed angle. If the first or bottom strip is shifted and the second strip is in straight line, the overall shape of the quilt is basically rectangular or square. However if the second or top strip is angled instead of the bottom strip, the overall shape of the quilt will be uniquely angled.

In addition, you are not limited to two strips of fabric per side of the quilt top. Use two small wedges instead of one on a side or position the wedges in a corner, covering them with contrasting outer strips. Also, consider using sheer, lamé or metallic fabrics for your wedges.

The angle position of the wedge on the quilt top makes a difference in the outer shape of the quilt.

quilt top

quilt top

151

3 Use a variety of wedges, corners and other angled shapes to form an irregular, but interesting, border. Arrange the shapes at random around the edges of the quilt top and secure with a blind hemstitch.

Passages of the Spirit, *detail. This quilt features a border of wedges and random angled shapes.*

Painless mitering

There is no easier way to miter borders than with my topstitch technique. This method works well for mitering any degree angle. Use it for adjoining border strips that are different widths. You'll achieve perfect results every time. If your design has double borders, construct one set at a time. Miter the inner borders first and then finish with the second set of borders.

1 Pin the adjoining border strips in place and overlap them crosswise. Each strip must be long enough to extend beyond the end of the other by at least ½".

2 With the tip of a fabric marking pencil placed exactly in the inside corner formed by the two strips, align the edge of a ruler next to the pencil and across the border strips so it spans from inside corner to the outside corner. The ruler's edge will be slightly off to one side to accommodate the tip of the pencil. Mark in a straight line to the opposite corner. Be sure to achieve an accurate corner-to-corner marking.

Align the ruler's edge corner-to-corner on the crossed strips and draw a straight, accurate line.

3 Trim the top border strip, leaving a ½" seam allowance on the outer edge of the marked line. Turn under the seam allowance on the marked line and press well.

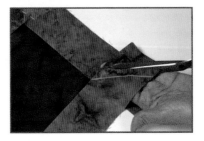

Turn under the seam allowance on the marked line.

4 Trace along the folded edge with a serrated tracing wheel. Gently fold back the top border strip from the corner. Trim the bottom border strip, leaving a generous ½" seam allowance on the outer edge of the indented line. Reposition the top border strip and pin in place. Use a blind hemstitch to sew the border.

Pin the mitered strip in place.

Explorations

"Bend" the rules of traditional thought—why does a mitered corner have to be a straight line? Try drawing a gentle "S" curved line from corner to corner instead. Clip valley curves and turn under the seam allowance as usual. Pin and blind hemstitch.

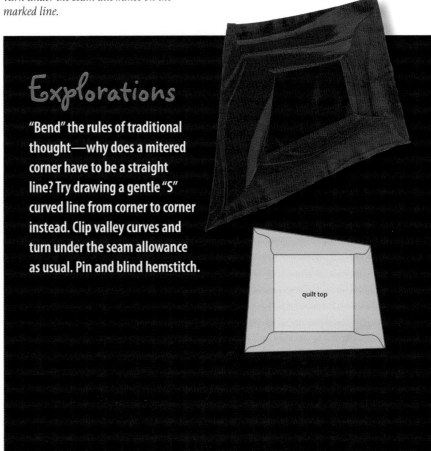

quilt top

Preparing the quilt top for finishing

Before the quilt is sandwiched and quilted, you must have an idea which technique you will use to finish the project. The quilt top is sandwiched differently depending on the finishing method you use. Batting is included as usual, but for the Envelope and Faux Binding finishes, a sheet of Pellon™ stabilizer is used in place of a backing fabric in this step. The quilting stitches will not show on the back of the quilt with these two techniques.

For the Faced Bindings (both front and back) the quilting will show on the back and the quilt. The quilt top is sandwiched with batting and a suitable backing fabric as usual.

Sandwiching the quilt top with Pellon™

Cut an ample sheet of Pellon™ stabilizer to use as the backing for the quilt sandwich. (See page 50 for enlarging stabilizer). Arrange the quilt sandwich with stabilizer on the bottom, batting or flannel in the middle and the quilt top, right side up, as the top layer. Do not stretch the Pellon™ backing when preparing and layering the sandwich. Pin with bent safety pins and quilt as desired.

Sandwiching the quilt top with backing fabric

Prepare the backing fabric by pressing well so it is perfectly flat and smooth. Sandwich the quilt by layering with the backing fabric on the bottom wrong side up (right side face down on the table), batting in the middle layer and the quilt top on the top surface, right side up.

I achieve the best results with my machine quilting when the backing fabric is stretched taut. To stretch the fabric backing on large quilts, center the backing fabric right side down on a cafeteria-type table. The fabric may extend over the edges of the table. Smooth the fabric, then use hand clamps to secure the fabric to the ends of the table, gently stretching the fabric just before clamping it. The fabric should be spread out firmly and evenly, not distorted out of shape.

Layer the batting on top of the backing fabric, smoothing the batting with your hands. Likewise, center and smooth the quilt top (right-side up) over the batting. Do not stretch the batting or quilt top. Use bent safety pins to join the layers at approximately 3-4" intervals. Work from the center out toward the edges, being sure all the layers are caught up in the pin. If necessary, reposition the clamps and quilt sandwich on the table and continue pinning the fringe areas of the sandwich.

Once the layers are secured, flip the quilt over to the back and inspect the backing fabric. Flatten and smooth the fabric with your hands from center out. The fabric should lie smoothly, even around the pin shaft. If there are crumples or excess material, remove the pin, smooth and re-pin. Quilt the quilt sandwich as desired.

153

Sandwiching back art

If you have created a backing piece with art or motifs, or "back art," you must determine the backing's center so you can position correctly and correspond it to the center of the quilt front. If the back art is simple, you can visually guesstimate the center. If the back art is a scene, or contains uneven or directionally extensive piecing, then you must first determine the approximate center. Lightly fold the backing piece in half, side to side, to determine where the vertical center line should be. Consider only the area intended for the back art and don't include excessive fabric around the perimeter. Make sure the backing's fold is smooth and does not twist or warp. Do not iron the fold. Simply pinch the fold at the top and at the bottom with your fingers to make a crease. Use a straight pin or fabric pencil to mark the creases on both the top and bottom edges on the front of the back art. Now fold the back art from top to bottom to determine the horizontal center line, crease and mark both sides.

In the same manner, find the horizontal and vertical center lines of your quilt top. Now measure and mark the center on all four sides of the cafeteria table (use drafting tape). When layering the backing piece for sandwiching, match the centers of the back art to the centers of the table on both ends and clamp. When layering the quilt top, correspond the marked centers of the quilt top with the centers of the back art. Be sure that the height marks or binding lines on your

backing hit close to the intended binding lines of the quilt top. Always double check the height and width positions before you start pinning the layers together. Check to make certain the layers are smooth and quilt the quilt sandwich as desired.

Back art of **Creation of the Sun and Stars**.

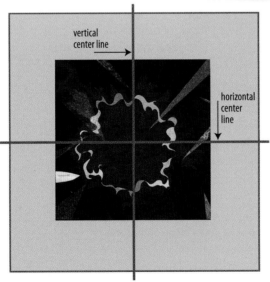

Mark the vertical and horizontal centers on the outer edges of the quilt back. This photo is the back art of **Passages of the Spirit.**

154

Finishing odd-shaped quilts

Finishing quilts can be a challenge, especially if you think outside the box to create an irregular or odd-shaped quilt with curves and angles. It would be impossible to bind a quilt like that with a traditional binding. One option is to finish the quilt with an envelope finish. The envelope finish is fast and easy. However, if you want the quilting to show on the back, or want to incorporate back art, a motif or scene, into the back of the quilt, the envelope option is not suitable.

In those instances, the perfect solution may be facing the quilt. With this technique, we will face the entire quilt with a whole piece of cloth and then cut away the center. This differs from dressmaking where the raw edges are faced with thin strips. This method does not waste cloth or money as the center is cut away as a single large piece, leaving the fabric intact and ready to use again in piecing or finishing another project. In addition, using a whole cloth rather than facing only the edges is much easier. There are no measurements to figure--difficult at best if the quilt has odd shapes and uneven angles and protrusions. Also, the end result with the whole cloth facing technique is an even and equal tension on every side, angle, protrusion and recess in the perimeter of the quilt. I use the whole cloth facing even for very large quilts.

Preparing the quilted sandwich for finishing

Once the quilt top is sandwiched and quilted, you must determine and mark the final outer shape on the quilt.

Remember as you consider the shape of your quilt that no longer are you restricted to square or rectangular quilts! With my finishing techniques you can virtually finish the quilt in any irregular shape or with any curvy or angular binding line. The following steps apply to all finishing techniques:

1 Decide on a pleasing final outer shape for the quilted quilt top. Mark the intended seam line with a fabric marking pencil on the quilt top. I'll refer to this as the "binding line".

2 *Now* is the easiest time to fix anything you missed during construction of the quilt top. If you added a new patch to improve the design, be sure there is a foundation of stabilizer and batting beneath the new patch. With any finishing technique you must have a stabilizer foundation large enough to catch the stitching when you apply the final backing fabric. If there is no stabilizer and batting under a section of stitching to provide rigidity, the binding seam will pucker. It doesn't matter how small the area in question—it will show. If the current foundation/batting layer falls short of

the binding line in places, simply add on to extend the layers. Cut a piece of stabilizer large enough to suffice and slip it beneath the stabilizer foundation so it straddles the existing layer and extends out far enough to cover the area needed. Straighten the edge of the batting and butt a new, straight-edged piece of batting against the first. The edges should fit closely but not overlap. Use a medium zigzag stitch to join the new foundation and batting to the original layer.

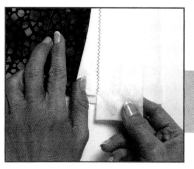

If the existing stabilizer/batting foundation falls short of the binding line on the quilt top, extend the foundation to cover the shortage. Without the stability the stabilizer provides, the finishing seam will pucker.

3 Closely inspect the entire quilt top, making sure there are no raw seams or edges just inside of the binding line. As you plot an exciting shape for your new quilt you may inadvertently extend the binding line beyond the end of a seam allowance joining two patches. It is very easy to miss seeing the raw edges, especially with dark fabrics. You definitely want to catch and correct this problem before you stitch the binding or facing fabric.

Machine basting the quilt perimeter

4 Thread your machine with a thread color that blends with the colors on the quilt top and a brightly colored thread in the bobbin. Using a large machine basting stitch, sew along the drawn binding line on the surface of the quilt top. The bright bobbin thread will be visible on either the stabilizer or fabric backing. Again, inspect for raw seams and unfinished edges along the binding line on the quilt top. For Envelope and Faux Binding finishes only, mark the top of the quilt with a straight pin. The pin's placement will help you find the top of the quilt once the backing is sewn on.

Envelope finish

Prepare the quilt sandwich with a stabilizer backing and prepare for finishing as directed in steps 1-4, page 155.

Choose a backing fabric that blends with the quilted quilt top. Lay the backing fabric face down on the quilt top, right sides together. Press. Pin so the backing fabric lies smoothly. With envelope finishes, it is important that the backing be as taut as possible, drawing the quilt surface to the back once it is turned inside out. This way, the backing fabric doesn't show on the front.

Note:

To achieve the tautness I need for large quilts, I stretch the envelope backing fabric right side up on a cafeteria-style table and secure the edges with hand clamps. Then the quilt top is placed right side down on the backing fabric and smoothed out, but not stretched. After pressing well, the layers are joined with safety pins.

The brightly colored basted binding line is visible on the stabilizer. Position the sewing machine needle just inside of the basting line and stitch around the perimeter. Sew with a consistent speed, especially around curves to achieve a smooth line. Even stretching the backing fabric on a table is no guarantee there will not be excess give in the backing after the perimeter is stitched. When using this technique with medium and larger quilts, I quickly learned that it's best to stitch the perimeter around three sides, stop and remove all the safety pins. Iron the back well, pressing and working the backing fabric evenly in the direction toward the unstitched area to eliminate the excess stretch in the fabric. Re-pin the unstitched perimeter and finish the stitching.

After stitching, inspect for jagged or uneven stitches. Restitch any questionable areas with another short line of stitching to smooth. If you leave jagged stitches, it does show when you turn the quilt inside out. To prevent a ridge after the quilt is turned inside-out, trim excess seam allowance to ⅜", then grade the seam by trimming one

seam allowance to ¼". Clip the valley curves.

Locate the straight pin you put in the topside of the quilt. Turn the quilt to the back and make a long slit in the backing fabric in the area that coincides with the placement of the quilt's hanging sleeve. When you make the slit take care not to nip the fabrics in quilt top beneath it. You may fuse snippets of fusible interfacing at each end of the slit to prevent the fabric from ripping further as you turn the quilt inside out. Turn the quilt inside out through the slit. Poke out and straighten the seam line with a plastic corner or blunt instrument. Press well with steam on both the front and the back of the quilt. I always use a press cloth to press the front of a completed quilt top.

Before you seal the slit in the backing, make another thorough examination of the quilt top.

• Inspect the areas around the perimeter for raw edges between patches. If you extended your binding line or inadvertently didn't notice a raw seam, you can return the quilt to the inside and re-stitch the area before you finish the quilt.

- Look for puckers in curves and deep "V" cuts. The puckers mean you didn't make the clips deep enough. Go back inside to make a deeper clip in the seam.

- Look for a smooth stitching line. Fix any glitches or jags that are visible.

- Be sure that all the curves in the seam line are fully extended or pushed out. Once the backing is sealed, it is almost impossible to adjust the seam line from the outside without compromising the fabric. I check this by carefully going over the seamed edge between the backing and quilt top on the outside of the quilt. Make sure you can see the thread/stitches from the inside seam. If you don't see evidence of thread

or a seamline, the curved seam is not completely pushed out.

Press to smooth the backing fabric one final time, moving the iron and any excess stretch in the fabric toward the slit area. If there is some excess, you may be able to conceal the ease with the hanging sleeve. Now that the quilt is turned inside out, checked and pressed flat, you are ready to seal the slit in the backing fabric.

If the backing fabric is lying flat and smooth, seal the slit closed with snippets of fusible webbing placed between the backing and stabilizer. Position the fusible webbing only in the slit area. Press to fuse.

If the quilt is large in size or the backing fabric seems too puffy even after sufficient ironing, use pieces of fusible webbing (sold

by the yard) to adhere the backing fabric to the stabilizer. Use the lightest weight or sheerest fusible you can for this step. Lay the quilt face down on a table. Reaching into the slit, insert the piece of fusible webbing between the wrong side of the backing fabric and the stabilizer. Press to fuse. Try to distribute the webbing as evenly as possible across the area. Work from the bottom of the quilt to the top and on one small area at a time. Please note that whenever you use a fusible, no matter how lightweight, some texture from the quilting on the back of the Pellon™ foundation will show on the backing fabric after fusing. This is inevitable. After the slit is sealed, cover it with the hanging sleeve. The sleeve and the name label, if you add one, will help secure the backing to the quilt top.

Explorations

Make a long slit in the top of the quilt and turn the quilt inside-out through the slit. Cover the slit with a hanging sleeve.

OR

If your project does not call for a hanging sleeve, you may cut the slit in backing fabric in an area where you can put a name label. Cut the backing fabric into a small "X" shape instead of the straight line. Turn the quilt inside out through the "X" slit. Seal and cover the slit with a name label.

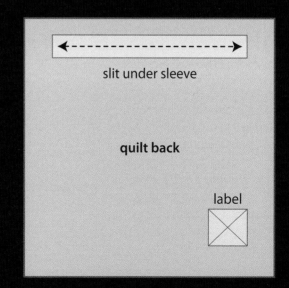

slit under sleeve

quilt back

label

The facing on the back of **Spirit of Joy.**

Binding Options

Faced binding finished to the back

For the faced binding finish, the quilt top is sandwiched with a suitable fabric backing layer and quilted.

Follow steps 1-4 on page 155 "Preparing the quilted sandwich for finishing." After machine basting the outer perimeter of the quilt, trim away the excess sandwich layer to about an inch out from the binding line.

Choose a fabric for the facing that complements and blends with the quilt top. Even though the facing will turn to the back of the quilt, you will be able to see a glimpse of the fabric around the very outside edge of the quilt at the seam line.

The amount of facing fabric you need depends on the size of the quilt. You'll need a piece of cloth large enough to cover the whole quilt and extend at least 1" beyond all binding lines. When considering fabric measurements and before cutting the facing fabric, keep in mind the facing fabric will be positioned right sides together with the quilt top. This is important to remember when working with odd-shaped quilts. Otherwise, the facing fabric will not match the shape of the quilt—it will be reversed.

Press the facing fabric well. For small quilts place the quilt face up on a table and cover it with the facing fabric so right sides are together. With your hands, smooth the fabric over the quilt and press with iron. Secure the two layers together in the center of the quilt with bent safety pins every 4" to 5" inches, but don't use safety pins

too close to the binding lines-they will get caught in the feed dogs of the sewing machine. Flip the quilt over and secure the areas around the binding line with straight pins.

I have successfully used whole cloth facing for very large quilts. You may choose either a fabric that is manufactured in a large width (such as 90") or you may sew two identical strips of 44" wide fabric together with a straight stitch. Press the seam open.

When layering the facing fabric on large quilts, stretch the facing fabric taut, right side up, on a cafeteria-style table and secure it with hand clamps. The quilt is positioned right side down on the facing fabric and the two layers joined with safety pins.

Reset your sewing machine to a short stitch length and thread the machine and bobbin with thread that blends with the quilt and facing. Turn the quilt to the back where you will see the colored thread basting line (as described on page 156). Position the sewing machine needle so it stitches just inside of the basting line. This will eliminate the need to remove the basting stitch. Stitch around the entire perimeter of the quilt using a consistent speed, especially around curves. Inspect the line of stitching and correct any jagged stitches. Trim the excess seam allowance close to the seam line to approximately ⅛" to ¼". Carefully clip all valley curves, making sure you do not clip the seam line. Turn over the quilt so the wrong side of the facing fabric is facing up.

With fabric scissors, make a slit in the facing fabric about three inches in from the seam line. Take care not to nip the face of the quilt top. Follow along the perimeter of the quilt, cutting away the center of the facing fabric from the quilt. You can cut farther away than three inches from the seam line, but never cut closer than two inches. Don't cut in a straight line, but with elongated and gentle waves. You may even intersperse angular shapes such as a mountain peak with an angle of 90° or more but I strongly suggest you do not incorporate deep "V" curves or angles. Modify them into gentle valley curves instead. Cut away the inside of facing fabric in one piece so that you

may reuse it for another facing in a smaller quilt or for patches in a quilt.

Cut away the facing fabric from the quilt in a curvy line. Don't cut any closer than 2" from the seam line.

Turn the facing fabric inside out to the back of the quilt. Use a blunt instrument or plastic corner to push out and straighten the seam line. Press well so the facing lays flat on the back of the quilt. Turn under the raw edge of the entire facing a little at a time, pressing with an iron and using straight pins to secure the facing to the quilt.

You may sculpt the curves you cut into the facing as you please. The curves will give a pretty, graceful look to the faced binding. You may include some gentle mountain angles if you wish but avoid deep "V" cuts. Lightly clip valley curves to get them to turn under properly. There are no rules as to how much fabric you should allow for the seam allowance or how wide you should make the facing on the back. For visual interest be sure to vary the width of the facing...wider in some areas, narrower in others. Some of my quilts have a wide facing up to 6" or 7" in some places but I've found from personal experience that I prefer narrower widths in facing (2"-3") and think it makes a better appearance.

Once the facing's seam allowance is turned under and secured and you are pleased with its curves and shape, whipstitch the facing by hand to the quilt back and add the hanging sleeve.

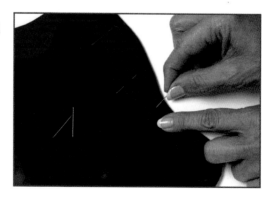

Turn facing to the back of the quilt. Clip valley curves and turn under a seam allowance.

Faced binding finished to the front

Constructed in a manner similar to the back facing, finishing a quilt using an innovative front facing gives the unusual appearance of having a graceful, asymmetrical frame around the quilt face. When making a quilt with a front facing, take into account that the facing will cover up some of the quilt's surface. Make allowances for that as you choose and construct the patches around the quilt perimeter and plot the binding line on the quilt top. This facing works well on all quilts but is especially fun with improvisational ones.

Follow the steps above for sandwiching, preparing and marking the quilt top as above. Use fabric as the backing layer for the quilt sandwich. Next, choose a fabric for the front facing that directly complements, blends or is one of the fabrics in your quilt top.

Press the facing fabric well. The next step is where the front facing technique differs from the back facing. Instead of placing the facing fabric face down on the quilt top as you did with the back facing, lay the facing fabric, right side down, on top of the quilt's backing fabric (right sides together). Smooth and pin the layers together as before. Stitch around the perimeter of the quilt, just inside of the basted binding line. Trim the excess sandwich layers close to the seam line and clip curves if needed.

Taking care not to accidentally cut the quilt's backing fabric, make a slit in the facing fabric at least 3" from the edge of the seam. Cut the facing in gentle waves all around the quilt. Turn facing inside out to the right side of the quilt top. Sculpt pleasing curves by turning under the raw edges of the facing, pressing and securing the seam with straight pins. Vary the width of the facing for visual appeal and even incorporate a few angles among the curves for more interest. Hand-stitch the facing to the quilt top. Add a hanging sleeve on the back.

Front facing on **Shooting Star**.

Faux binding

This technique gives a quilt the illusion of having a unique and wild-shaped binding. In fact, the "binding" is actually a moderately thin curvy-shaped contrasting border that you add to the quilt top after the quilting is completed. You will design and mark each side of the quilt with an initial binding line. A border strip is created from the initial binding line. After the curvy border strips are constructed and stitched to the quilt top, you will mark a secondary curvy binding line on the outer edges of the sewn border strips. For visual interest, the second binding line is shaped differently than the first. You'll complete the quilt with an envelope finish.

As with any binding that shows on the front of a quilt, you must choose an appropriate fabric that quietly complements the quilt and doesn't overpower or take over as the center of interest. With *Oriental Poppy*, I chose a hand-dyed fabric that contained the colors that were in my quilt, but had sufficient contrast in value from the quilt's background. I wanted to bring out the deepest violet color I'd put in the poppy's center and the narrow strips in the background folds. I've found from experience that adding some focal point color (in this case the poppy) somewhere into the quilt's border or binding helps to balance the quilt and enhance the focal point. The fabric I used for my faux binding contained both deep purple and dark red-orange and was the perfect choice.

In my opinion, keeping the width of the border in the narrow range in relation to the overall size of the quilt gives the best results. You will design a second, final binding line that is totally different from the first one, meaning the width of the border will vary from one area to the next depending on your design. On *Oriental Poppy*, the border widths range from ½" in some places to 2½" in others. This variance in width makes for an interesting binding.

Sandwich the quilt top with batting and stabilizer instead of backing fabric. Quilt and prepare the quilt for finishing as instructed in steps 1-3 on page 155. Design a pleasing shape, using a fabric pencil to mark the initial binding line on the quilt top. The more unusual the shape of the binding line, the more exciting the final outcome. For inspiration as you create the shapes for the binding line, look for some of the shapes and lines within the quilt's design or focal point and echo them in your binding. Add waves, wide V shapes (inverted V as well) and/or scallops.

The faux binding on **Oriental Poppy** *is an easily accomplished illusion.*

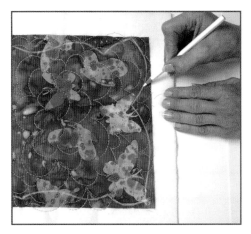

Mark the initial binding line on the quilt.

To begin the faux binding process you will construct the border using my regular curves technique and freezer paper. You must transfer the shape of the binding line, one side of the quilt at a time, to freezer paper in order to create a template. Then you can accurately cut out the border fabric and turn under the seam allowance. The very best way to do this is:

•Cut a freezer paper border strip for one side of the quilt top. The size you cut the strip depends on the intended size of the border. Generally I cut a piece of freezer paper the length of the quilt's side plus an additional 3" for mitering (optional) on each corner. The width of the paper strip depends on the intended width of the border but I prefer to cut a generous width, about 6" to 8" and cut away the excess. Remember the width will vary and you need to take into account seam allowances on both long sides of the border.

•Lay the quilt, right side up, on a soft surface such as a padded ironing board or a table covered with a towel or layer of batting. Insert the strip of freezer paper, shiny side down, between the soft surface and the quilt. Sandwich the freezer paper between the soft surface and the quilt top so the inside edge of the freezer paper strip extends and lies beneath the entire binding line about ¾", leaving most of the strip width on the outside.

•Next trace the marked initial binding line with a serrated tracing wheel. Without a soft surface, the indentations from the tracing wheel will not show up on the freezer paper. Use moderate pressure as you trace. Lift up the edge of the quilt to see if you are transferring the image. The little teeth in the tracing wheel should leave indentations in the freezer paper and you should have a pretty close rendering of the binding line embedded in the paper.

Use a serrated tracing wheel to trace the initial binding line and make a freezer paper template. Mark the edge to be turned under with arrows and construct the template as usual.

•Remove the freezer paper and cut the freezer paper template along the indented line. This is the top edge of your border template. Mark the cut, indented edge of paper template with little arrows and the word, "top". You will turn under the seam allowance on this edge marked with arrows and align it with the initial binding line on the quilt.

•Place the paper template on the right side of the border fabric and press. Cut out the border patch, leaving seam allowance on both long edges. Note that when you cut out the patch from the border fabric, you are focusing on the top edge to be turned under. There is no specific bottom edge yet since you have not drawn the secondary binding line. Also, the width of your freezer paper will vary depending on where you placed it when you traced the binding line. When you cut out the fabric patch, be sure you leave enough width on the bottom of the strip to make a sufficiently wide border. Clip valley curves on the top marked edge and turn under the seam allowance as usual. Position on the quilt surface and pin.

•Continue these steps with the remaining sides of the quilt. Machine blind hemstitch the border strips to the quilt top. Press well.

162

Once the border strips are sewn, design a secondary binding line for each side of the quilt top.

Mark the secondary binding line on the border strip. This secondary binding line is also the final perimeter of the quilt. Again, include waves, wide V shapes (inverted V as well) and/or scallops into the design. Once the secondary binding line is marked on the quilt, machine baste on the secondary binding line (perimeter) of the quilt top as directed on page 156, step 4. Finish the faux binding with an envelope finish as directed on page 156.

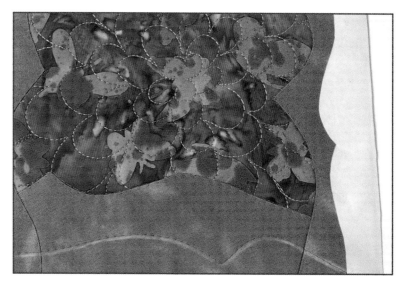

Mark the secondary binding line on all sides of the quilt. Machine baste the outline using a large stitch.

Explorations

1 Many times I "cheat" on this step by using the same freezer paper templates as I did when constructing the initial binding line. If the spirit moves me, I'll make a few minor trimming adjustments to the shapes in the binding line here and there. Since you only need the binding line portion of the template, I trim away the most of the bottom edge from the freezer paper template, leaving approximately an inch or two of the top edge (with the arrows). Turn the templates around so the edge with the small arrows faces outward and reposition the templates on different sides of the quilt and press. Machine baste around the perimeter of the quilt, using the freezer paper template as a guideline.

2 For total freedom, improvisationally design and draw the border strips directly on the freezer paper rather than mark the perimeter of the quilt. Make several different freezer paper templates. Cut them from freezer paper and position the templates on the quilt to see how they fit.

Hanging sleeve with easement

This is the technique I use for making a hanging sleeve. It allows some ease for large hanging rods (especially in shows and competitions) and helps the quilt to hang better.

Back of **Engulfed.**

Hang the finished quilt, top surface facing you, on your design wall. Decide on the best position for the quilt—how it looks and hangs the best. Even though you are working on the front surface, determine where the top of the sleeve should align on the back. Use a long level to achieve a straight line and to determine exact measurements. I generally allow one to two inches down from the top of the quilt. Mark these measurements on the front surface using straight pins.

Turn the quilt over to the back and pin on the design wall. Using the pins as a guide, level the quilt on the design wall. Use a marking pencil and level to mark a line across the top of the quilt. This line will help you align your finished sleeve to the quilt. Remove the straight pins from the front of the quilt.

Before you make the sleeve, you need to determine the sleeve measurements. A single sleeve spanning the width of the quilt works well for most quilts. However if you are attaching a sleeve to a quilt with openings, you may need to construct the sleeve in two or three segments so the sleeve doesn't interfere with the openings or the hanging rod doesn't show. Segments can be staggered across the quilt back to accommodate the openings in the quilt. If the sleeve segments are placed between openings, make sure they are positioned high enough above the openings (about two inches or so) so that a hanging rod does not show through the openings when it is slipped through the sleeve. Each segment can vary in width depending on its placement and the area available for a sleeve on the quilt back.

The segments should be the same length, generally 4-5 inches to accommodate hanging rods. Most quilt competitions and shows ask for at least a 4" sleeve, but for smaller quilts or those destined for home use, you may prefer a narrower length. Double that measurement and add one inch. Next measure the width across the top of the quilt to determine a width for the sleeve.

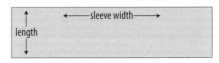

If the top shape of the quilt is irregular, measure the narrowest point. I usually use that measurement when I cut the sleeve fabric. Once the seam allowances are turned under, the sleeve should fit to within 1½" from the edge of the quilt. If you are constructing the sleeve in segments or don't want the sleeve to extend all the way to the edge, add 3" for the seam allowance to your measurement for each segment. Cut the sleeve strip from the appropriate fabric and press.

With the wrong side of the fabric facing up, turn up ¾" (wrong sides will be together) on each short side of the sleeve and press well. Tack seam allowance in place with some bits of fusible web if desired. Turn over each edge a second time at ¾" and press to set a crease in the fabric, and then unfold. Do not tack down the second fold.

164

Turn under a ¾" seam allowance twice on the short edge of the sleeve and press well. After pressing in the crease, unfold the second allowance.

Fold sleeve in half lengthwise, right sides together, so the long edges match exactly. Stitch the seam across the long length of the sleeve, making a tube. Use a ½" seam allowance. Press the long seam open. Refold the ¾" seam allowance (on the crease) on each short end of the sleeve and press.

Turn the sleeve right side out. Adjust the needle position on your machine to the farthest left position, placing the needle almost to the inside edge, catching the turned seam allowance. Topstitch around the openings on both sides of the sleeve.

Fold the sleeve (right side out) lengthwise (long edges) so the seam is positioned exactly in the center of the tube. Make sure the seam is centered straight. Press well. Using the longest machine basting stitch, sew a ½" seam along the top folded edge.

After stitching the long sides, refold the ¾" on the short sides and topstitch.

Baste a ½" seam along the edge of the sleeve to the right of the centered seam.

Refold the sleeve again, this time with the sleeve's main seam on the bottom of the sleeve and the basted seam in the center. Iron the sleeve well, pressing the basted seam down. With the basted seam facing outward and the main seam on the bottom, align the top of the sleeve to the previously marked placement line on the quilt back and pin well. Hand-stitch the top and bottom of the sleeve to the quilt. Once the sleeve is sewn down on both long edges, remove the basting stitches and press again. The ease in the sleeve will allow the quilt to hang smoother.

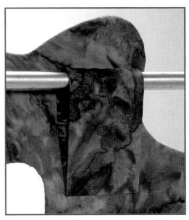

Hanging sleeve with easement allows the quilt to hang better on a rod.

I've given you many options for unique borders and finishing techniques in this chapter. The artistic potential for utilizing improvisational borders in your quilts is limitless, and designing and finishing a quilt with unusual edges or irregularly shaped perimeters has never been easier. You are no longer "bound" to squares or rectangles for your projects, so give yourself the freedom to think unconventionally. Explore all the paths and possibilities!

English Ivy

Enlarge 250%

166

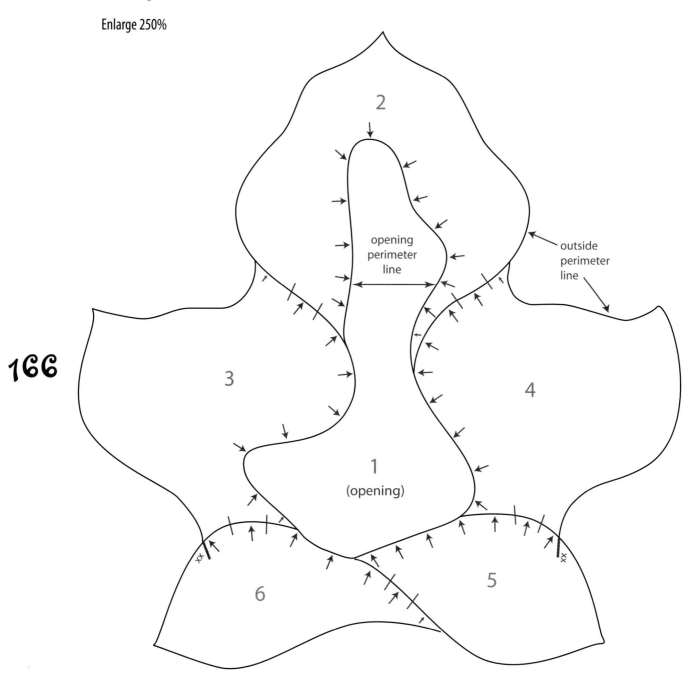

2

opening
perimeter
line

outside
perimeter
line

3

4

1
(opening)

6

5

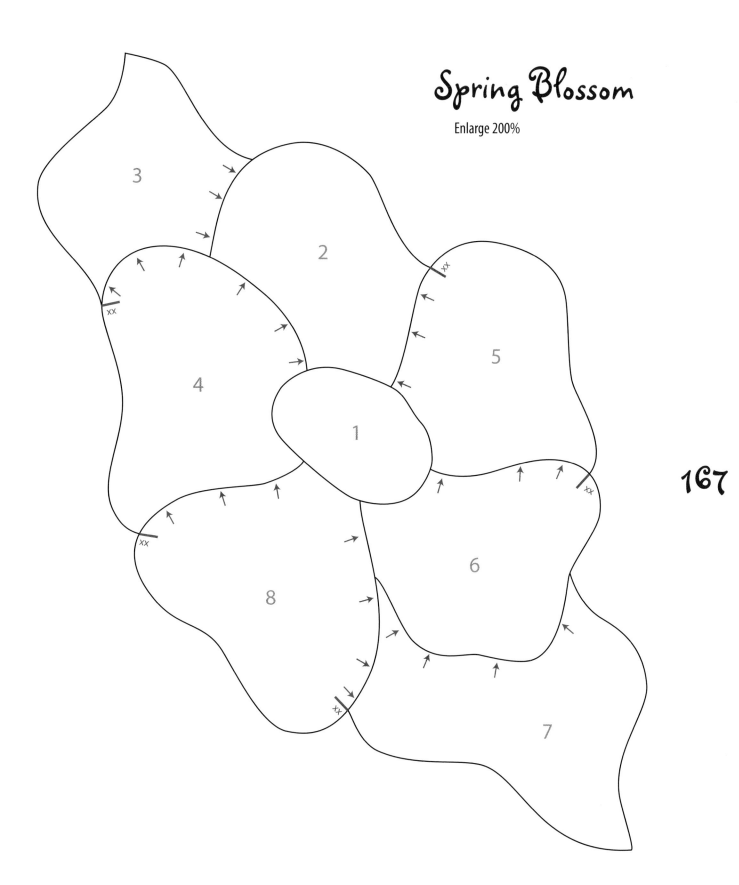

Spring Blossom

Enlarge 200%

167

My Star Dances

Enlarge 200%

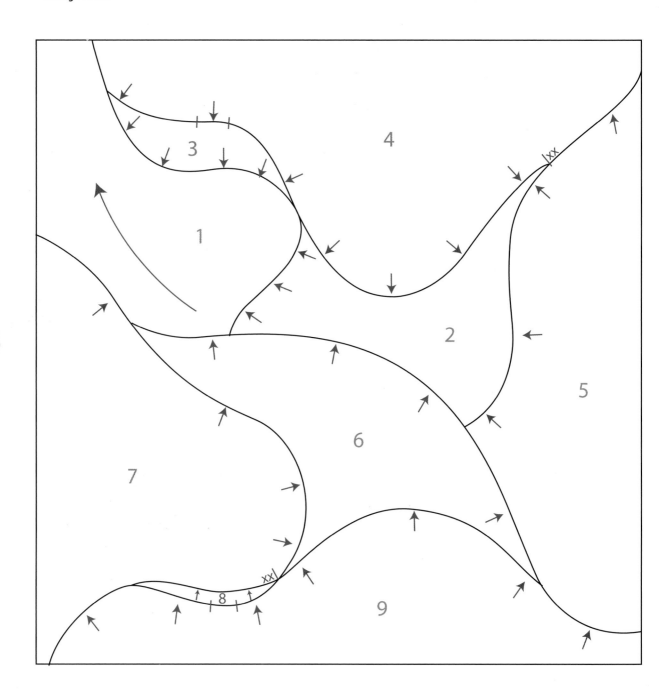

QUILTING BY IMPROVISATION

Resources

Benartex Fabrics
1359 Broadway
STE 1100
New York, NY 10018

Bernina
Sewing machines
3702 Prairie Lake Ct.
Aurora, IlL 60504
800-877-0477
www.berninausa.com

Bold Over Batiks!
Batik fabrics
458 Warwick St.
St. Paul, MN 55105
651-917-0432
www.boldoverbatiks.com

The Crowning Touch
Fasturn™ / tube turning tools
3859 South Stage Road
Medford, OR 97501

Dragon Threads
Publisher
490 Tucker Dr.
Worthington, OH 43085
614-841-9388
www.dragonthreads.com

Fabri-quilt
Fabrics
901 E. 14th Ave
North Kansas City, MO 64116

Fairfield Processing Corporation
Batting
88 Rose Hill Ave
Danbury, CT 06813
www.poly-fil.com

Heritage Cutlery, Inc
Scissors
7971 Refinery Rd.
Bolivar, New York 14715
www.heritagecutlery.com

Hoffman California Fabrics
25792 Obrero Dr.
Mission Viejo, CA 92691
www.hoffmanfabrics.com

Janome
Sewing Machines
10 Industrial Ave.
Mahwah, NJ 07430
201-825-3200
www.janome.com

Just Imagination
Judy Robertson hand-dyed fabrics
P.O. Box 83
Bow, WA 98232
360-766-4030
www.justimagination.com

OESD
Aqua Mesh™
water-soluble stabilizer
12101 I-35 Service Rd.
Oklahoma City, OK 73131
www.oesd.com

OLFA-North America
Rotary cutters, mats, rulers
5500 N. Pearl St, Suite 400
Rosemont, IL 60018
800-962-OLFA
www.olfarotary.com

Pellon Consumer Products
Stabilizer
2000 Jabco Blvd.
Lithonia, GA 30058
800-516-5774

Vikki Pignatelli
6620 Forrester Way
Reynoldsburg, OH 43068
www.vikkipignatelli.com
vikkip@juno.com

Prym Consumer USA, Inc.
Dritz Notions
Spartanburg, NC
www.dritz.com

Quilters Dream Cotton
Batting
589 Central Dr.
Virginia Beach, VA 23454

Rowenta
Irons
196 Boston Ave.
Medford, MA
www.rowentausa.com

Sacred Threads Exhibitions
Biannually
www.exhibit-sacredthreads.com

Superior Threads
Box 1672
St George, UT 84771
www.superiorthreads.com

169

About the Author

170

A self-taught artist with experience in painting (watercolor and oils) and sculpture, Vikki enjoys a passion for color and flowing designs. She developed a simple layering technique that is a blend of piecing and appliqué and is the subject of her first book in 2001, *Quilting Curves* (Quilt Digest Press). Also, Vikki has written "how-to" articles published in Quilter's Newsletter and AQS magazines.

Vikki is the founder (1999) and co-chairwoman of the national biennial Sacred Threads Quilt Exhibitions, a two-week display of original artwork that explores themes of spirituality, joy, inspiration, healing and grief. The show is held in Reynoldsburg, Ohio.

Deeply influenced by her husband's bout with cancer and his recovery in 1993, most of Vikki's artwork now focuses on the themes of healing, spirituality, hope, and inspiration. In her writings and teaching, Vikki's focus is to inspire, nurture and develop the artistry and self-confidence within each quilter.

Vikki lives in Reynoldsburg, Ohio, with her husband of 38 years, Denny. They have two children, Denise and Dan. Vikki and her husband love to travel and dance for relaxation.

Vikki entered the world of quilting in 1991 at the urging of her sister, Augustine Ellis. A non-sewer at the time, Vikki attended a beginner's class and quickly fell in love with the art of quilting. Now a full-time professional quilt-artist, designer, international teacher, lecturer and author, Vikki and her quilts have been featured in many books, national publications and exhibitions. She has won numerous awards in national and international competitions and exhibitions.

At Sea

Awards

2006

Quilts For A Change
Cincinnati, OH
1st place
Passages of the Spirit

12th Annual Quiltfest
Pigeon Forge, TN,
1st Place, Professional
Passages of the Spirit

2005

The Appliqué Society Show
Best Color Award
Passages of the Spirit

The Appliqué Society Show
1st Place
Passages of the Spirit

The Appliqué Society Show
2nd Place
Engulfed

National Quilting Association Annual Show
Best Innovative Design
The Spider's Web

National Quilting Association Annual show
3rd place
The Spider's Web

The Minnesota Quilters Show
3rd Place
The Promise of Spring

The Minnesota Quilters Show
Faculty's Choice
The Promise of Spring

2004:

Form, Not Function Quilt Art Exhibit as the Carnegie Center of Art and History
New Albany, IN
Best of Show
Engulfed

Minnesota Quilt Show & Conference
Judges Choice
Engulfed

Minnesota Quilt Show & Conference
Honorable Mention
Engulfed

Quilter Guild of Dallas Quilt Show
2nd Place
Passages of the Spirit

Quilter Guild of Dallas Quilt Show
2nd Place
Life Beyond

2003

Minnesota Quilt Show & Conference
1st Place
Passages of the Spirit

National Quilting Association
Judges Recognition
Engulfed

2002

National Quilting Association
Best Color & Design
Passages of the Spirit

National Quilting Association
2nd Place
Passages of the Spirit

2001

Minnesota Quilt Show & Conference
Award #1, Faculty's Choice
Resting Place

Minnesota Quilt Show & Conference
Award #2, Faculty's Choice
Resting Place

Minnesota Quilt Show & Conference
3rd Place
Life Beyond

National Quilting Association
Honorable Mention
Creation of the Sun and Stars

2000

Homestead Invitational Quilt Exhibit
Rio Grande, OH
Peoples Choice Award
After the Storm

1999

Minnesota Quilt Show & Conference
2nd Place
The Fire Within

Minnesota Quilt Show & Conference
Faculty's Choice
After the Storm

172

1997

International Quilt Festival
Houston, TX
1st Place Art, large
Portrait of My Soul

International Quilt Festival
Houston, TX
Honorable Mention Art, small
After the Storm

**Pennsylvania National Quilt
Extravaganza**
1st Place
Portrait Of My Soul

**Minnesota Quilters Quilts On
The Waterfront**
Best Machine Quilting
Tears On Blacklick Pond

**Minnesota Quilters Quilts On
the Waterfront**
3rd Place
*Blacklick Pond Reflections At
Twilight*

Vermont Quilt Festival
2nd Place
Portrait Of My Soul

Mid-Atlantic Quilt Festival....
Honorable Mention
Tears On Blacklick Pond

Vermont Quilt Festival
3rd Place
*Blacklick Pond-Reflections At
Twilight*

**Pennsylvania National Quilt
Extravaganza**
Best Amateur Entry-Innovative
Fire and Ice

173

Tropical Totem

Artist's Statements

The Promise of Spring
As a gentle Spring breeze dances across Blacklick Pond, it coaxes the promise of new life from the branches of the Weeping Willow. *The Promise of Spring* represents the reawakening of earthly life after winter and the remembrance of life that has ceased to exist in our world (the ghost branches) but is revived after death in the life beyond.

The Spider's Web
Quilt is machine appliquéd. The web is handmade contemporary lace knotted with perle cotton threads and thin yarns. The texture on the quilt surface is a machine-made lace of alpaca fleece, threads and yarns secured with free-motion stitching.

Engulfed
I felt an intense urge to create this work. It wasn't until after I finished the quilt that I realized it was symbolic of my current emotional state! I was feeling weary, overburdened and "burned out." The hectic schedules and the constant busyness in my life was taking its toll. This quilt provided a sudden insight for me. It is a startling wake-up call to take more time to relax.

174

Creation of the Sun and Stars
God's omnipresent power, represented by the yellow ribbons, flows from all corners of the heavens to form our sun, the cranberry orb. As the newly-born sun spins, fire and flames are thrown back into the universe, eventually transforming into dancing stars.

Passages of the Spirit
Earthly life is plagued with struggles and human frailties, symbolized in this quilt with somber background colors: red (anger); green (jealousy, hopelessness); gray (anxiety); blue (sadness); and purple (sorrow). The broken jagged points are discord and conflict. My faith is that in the next life I'll conquer these failings and my purer spirit will transform into joy (yellow), love (pink), hope (green), serenity (blue) and spirituality (violet) in the presence of my Creator (gold).

Summer's Bounty
This artwork is inspired by one of nature's favorite wildflowers, the sunflower, which blooms profusely in mid-to-late summer.

Rhapsody In Pink
One of my favorite things in nature is seeing water lilies and lily pads floating in a pond. I imagine them to be alive and dancing with joy, swaying to the music of the gentle breeze.

Valley Of Fire
43"w x 33"h

Cabbage Rose
22¼"w x 21"h

Stairway to the Gods
37½"w x 29"h

Running in Circles
43" diameter

Field Poppies
46"w x 38"h

The Promise of Spring
62"w x73"h

Passages of the Spirit
72¼"w x 69"h

The Spider's Web
37"w x 47"h

Engulfed
42"w x 76"h

Summer's Bounty
30" diameter

At Sea
28"w x 36"h

Hanging On for Dear Life
23"w x 17"h

Spring Blossom
19½"w x 11"h

English Ivy
16"w x 17"h

Sunflower
16"w x 21½"h

Augie's Quilt
25"w x 38"h

Rosemary's Garden
34"w x 33"h

Pink Tulip
15½" x 20"h

Winter's Hostage
16"w x 19"h

Spirit of Joy

For the Love of Thais
38"w x 56"h

Dreamcatcher
24"w x 27"h

Windows
19"w x 38"h

Creation of the Sun and Stars
75"w x 65"h

Spirit of Joy
24" x 24"

Rhapsody In Pink
36"w x 32"h

Oriental Poppy
29"w x 32"h

Entwined
23"w x 21"h

He Loves Me, He Loves Me Not
27" x 27"

Sunrise Silhouette
19½"w x 20½"h

On Pins and Needles
44"w x 26½"h

Shooting Star
12½"w x 11"h

Passing Fancy
18"w x 13"h

My Star Dances
21"w x 15"h

Tropical Totem
21¼"w x 83"h

175

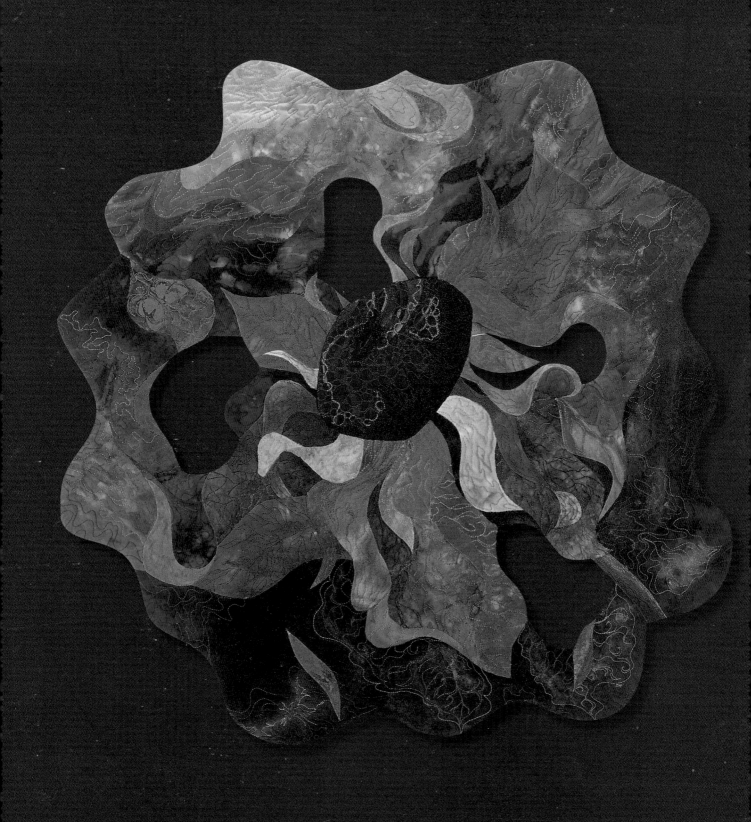

Summer's Bounty